"If leadership is defined by the influence you have on another, then Bobbie Houston is at the top of her game. Her longevity and credibility as a leader is only surmounted by her passion and focus to see heaven come to Earth through the extraordinary love of Christ in ordinary people. *Stay the Path* will give you invaluable insight into her miraculous journey of godly leadership."

—John C. Maxwell, author and leadership expert

"Life is a daring adventure full of opportunities, obstacles, challenges, disappointments, and victories. We each have our own lane in this race we are called to run; *Stay the Path* by Bobbie Houston provides a powerful, practical, and inspirational road map on how to navigate the endless twists and turns of life so that you can fulfill your God-given destiny. Wisdom gained over decades of faithfulness, steadfastness, commitment, and tenacity is precious and priceless, and I'm grateful that Bobbie has penned these pages. She shares her journey with grace and strength, and champions us all to run our race and to finish our course. This is a book that I will keep on my bookshelf and refer to over and over again."

—Christine Caine, founder of A21

"This is a very powerful message, rooted in biblical principles, that every believer can benefit from, especially with the current issues and circumstances we are facing around the world today. I'm excited to see how God is using Bobbie Houston to help strengthen Christians in their faith."

—Joyce Meyer, Bible teacher and bestselling author

"A lot of people start strong, but few finish strong. If there is anyone who can teach you how to run your race and finish well, it's Pastor Bobbie Houston. Her important new book, *Stay the Path*, is full of wisdom, warmth, and depth that will encourage you to do the right things today so you'll end up at the right place in the future. My family is thankful for Bobbie's example. We are different and better because we have learned from her. You will be too."

—Craig and Amy Groeschel, pastors of
Life.Church and authors of
From This Day Forward

"With simplicity and relatable warmth, Bobbie shares some of the challenges and experiences that shaped her life as a woman in leadership at Hillsong Church. *Stay the Path* will tug at your heartstrings and challenge you to create strongholds that will help you have unshakable faith in the face of adversity."

—Kay and Rick Warren, founders of
Saddleback Church

"Our friend Bobbie Houston is a wordsmith, and as such her book *Stay the Path* is at once poetic and prophetic. Each page of this captivating read is an invitation to weigh your life in the eternal balance and lead as the One we were told to follow would. Pastor Bobbie's dearest desire is to see men and women, young and old, finish the course that God has laid out for them in wisdom and strength."

—John and Lisa Bevere, founders of Messenger
International and bestselling authors

"This is my mum. She is the most extraordinary person I know. If she were president of Earth, Earth would look a whole lot more like the kingdom of heaven. If anyone has anything to say about journey and process, it is my mum. She emits the way of Jesus like no one I know. (No offense, Dad.) But you would only be moving closer to Jesus to read this book."

—**Joel Houston, songwriter and worship leader, Hillsong UNITED**

"We all need someone encouraging us who is just a little ahead on the journey, and my dear friend Bobbie will be that someone for you. I have been friends with Bobbie for over twenty years and have watched her live out her faith with such genuineness. Step-by-step she has been faithful to walk the leadership path she has been entrusted with. In *Stay the Path*, using her friendly yet poetic communication style, she describes challenges and victories, and at the same time gives us the practical how-to we all need as we walk the journey God has trusted us with. This is an inspirational as well as practical leadership guide. You might just need to get one for a friend too!"

—**Holly Wagner, pastor of Oasis Church and author of *Find Your Brave***

"In a generation that has elevated fame over faithfulness and temporary accolade over eternal treasure, *Stay the Path* is a much needed wake-up call. This book shakes us out of the doldrums of spiritual lethargy and snatches us from the brink of throwing in the towel. It reminds us that the virtues of honor, consistency, integrity, and longevity are still valuable and necessary. Thank you for this book, Bobbie, and for illustrating its message with a life well lived."

—**Priscilla Shirer, Bible teacher and author**

"Experience in and of itself, is overrated. I've heard it said, 'If you want to know the truth, ask somebody who has been there.' That is only true if they have already been there EFFECTIVELY... that's why I love Bobbie, that's why I'm glad she is my pastor, and that's why I look to her example of 'staying on the path' while I try to navigate my own... She continues to do it right! Impacting countless people on the way. There has never been a more confusing time in culture with almost endless 'paths' to choose from. But only one path leads to LIFE and it begins and ends with Jesus. That is the only path Bobbie has ever pointed to, has ever championed, and has ever promoted. This book will truly illuminate the RIGHT path and eliminate some wrong paths as well. One thing is for sure, I will be strategically placing this book 'in the paths' of many, because I don't want to see anybody lose their way. I can't wait to see the impact it has on those I love!"

—**Carl Lentz, lead pastor of Hillsong NYC**

"Bobbie is an inspiring leader who has not only written but lived out the reality of 'Staying the Path' in every aspect of her life. I highly recommend this book to anyone who desires a lasting vision for their life and ministry. I have no doubt that you will be greatly encouraged by her genuine love for the church and for God's precious people."

—**Joseph Prince, senior pastor of New Creation Church**

"Bobbie Houston is the perfect model of one who has stayed on the path with Jesus. She is a woman, wife, mother, and church leader who has shown us all what God can do. Bobbie makes it look so easy but her path has been anything but. Her faith, strength, and love keep her going through every challenge. You will be encouraged and empowered by *Stay the Path*."

—**Casey and Wendy Treat, senior pastors of Christian Faith Center, Seattle**

"Thank you for writing this book! Bobbie Houston's remarkable life journey has forged a treasure of wisdom and a heartfelt passion to inspire and encourage you to stay true on your own unique path in God's purposes. Wonderfully relatable, *Stay the Path* serves up Bobbie's signature candor and warmth, and tells of a tested but resilient faith in the God who leads her."

—**Sy Rogers, teaching pastor and global communicator**

"Bobbie Houston is an extraordinarily faithful attendant of revelation, a devoted steward of what the Lord has entrusted to her, a passionate lover of Jesus Christ, and an unapologetic publisher of His praise—not for a couple of years or a fleeting season but year after year, decade after decade. Her longevity speaks volumes—not simply her longevity in ministry and leadership but her longevity in devotion, her longevity in servanthood, her longevity in passion and unwavering commitment to Christ, His Church, His Word, and this broken world for whom He came. I'm so grateful Bobbie has written this book—utterly grounded in reality while forward-reaching in faith—that gives all of us a glimpse into how she has so gracefully 'stayed the path' so that we might too."

—**Brooke Ligertwood, songwriter and worship leader, Hillsong Worship**

"Whether you are a pathfinder or someone that is content to walk along trails that others have blazed, this book will speak to your heart. You will be encouraged, challenged, and comforted as you read these words from the heart of someone that has 'stayed the path.'"

—**Bayless Conley, founding pastor of Cottonwood Church**

"In every generation God gifts us with those who see the big picture of what He is doing in our world. Pastor Bobbie is one of those visionaries. Not only has she walked out her calling with faithfulness, tenacity, and trust, now she shares that journey with us. God is on the move!"

—**Sheila Walsh, Bible teacher and author**

STAY *the* PATH

Navigating the Challenges and
Wonder of Life, Love, and Leadership

• • •

Bobbie Houston

SHOUT!
PUBLISHING

First published in the U.S.A. by FaithWords
A division of Hachette Book Group, Inc.

First published in Australia in 2017 by SHOUT! Publishing
ABN:37 002 745 879
PO Box 1195, Castle Hill, NSW 1765, Australia
shoutpublishing.com

The publisher is not responsible for websites (or their content) that are not owned by the publisher.

Scriptures are taken from the ESV® Bible (The Holy Bible, English Standard Version®). Copyright © 2001 by Crossway, a publishing ministry of Good News Publishers. Used by permission. All rights reserved.

Scriptures noted (AMP) are taken from the Amplified Bible. Copyright © 1954, 1958, 1962, 1964, 1965, 1987 by The Lockman Foundation. Used by permission. (www.lockman.org)

Scriptures noted (AMPC) are taken from the Amplified Bible, Classic Edition.

Scriptures noted (KJV) are taken from the King James Version of the Holy Bible.

Scriptures noted (MSG) are taken from The Message. Copyright © 1993, 1994, 1995, 1996, 2000, 2001, 2002. Used by permission of NavPress Publishing Group.

Scriptures noted (NHEB) are taken from the New Heart English Bible.

Scriptures noted (NIV) are taken from THE HOLY BIBLE, NEW INTERNATIONAL VERSION®, NIV®. Copyright © 1973, 1978, 1984, 2011 by Biblica, Inc.® Used by permission. All rights reserved worldwide.

Scriptures noted (NKJV) are taken from the New King James Version®. Copyright © 1982 by Thomas Nelson. Used by permission. All rights reserved.

Scriptures noted (YLT) are taken from Young's Literal Translation.

"With Everything"
Words and music by Joel Houston
© 2008 Hillsong Music Publishing

"Prince Of Peace"
Words and music by Joel Houston, Matt Crocker & Dylan Thomas
© 2015 Hillsong Music Publishing

"Mountain"
Words and music by Matt Crocker & Joel Houston
© 2012 Hillsong Music Publishing

Library of Congress Cataloging-in-Publication Data has been applied for.

ISBN: 978-1-4789-7525-0 (international trade paperback), 978-1-4555-9253-1 (ebook)

Printed in Australia

LSC-C

10 9 8 7 6 5 4 3 2 1

This book is dedicated to my grandchildren—Savannah, Lexi, Bailey, Willow, Zion, Jack, and Blaze (and any more who may one day join our family) in whom I see so much life, energy, personality, potential, and wonder. While only young now, they're going to grow up and become the future influencers of society and culture.

My prayer is that those who surround them in life will live within a stunning revelation of what life is truly about, and that in doing so, they'll fuel the walk and calling of these beautiful young lives. My prayer is that they will discover the path God has purposed for them and that they'll walk with confidence and boldness.

And to Brian Houston—so much of my own insight and wisdom within these pages has been learned alongside you as we've walked this forty-year journey together. You are an exceptional husband, father, friend, Poppa, visionary leader, and shepherd soul. Thank you.

FOREWORD

Bobbie and I are different—VERY DIFFERENT. I am full of vision, but have patience only for the headlines. I'm not sure that is a good confession; I suppose it is often a prevailing male trait. Bobbie, on the other hand, is visionary with endless patience for the details. I've heard it said that "the love is in the details." If this is true, then much of the details and excellence exemplified in our ministry is because it matters to Bobbie.

When I first laid eyes on her at a summer church convention on the east coast of New Zealand's North Island, I knew she was the one I wanted to travel life with. Her shy seventeen-year-old demeanor didn't mask a tangible love for the Savior she had just met. She had had a life-changing encounter with Christ and her wholehearted desire to serve God is what made me fall all the more in love with her.

In the early years of pioneering our ministry together, she was happy to remain behind the scenes, yet I have memories of her faithfully and tirelessly working to create a sense of "welcome home" for everyone who entered both our own home and our church home. In many ways she was the "reluctant leader"—happy to remain in the background yet never failing to develop capacity as a woman of God and forerunner within our sphere of influence. I have loved watching God trust her to speak into the heart and soul of our ministry and steward with me the many directives that have become clear distinctives within the life of Hillsong. She has always been and remains a steadying force in our family, a compass for our—now adult—children, and a rock that we can all rely upon.

Our forty-year journey hasn't been without challenge. Like everyone, we have faced the dynamics that come with the various seasons of life and pastoring—yet it has been my wife who has found redemption along the way, and therefore beauty in the journey. Her walk might be more whimsical than mine, but her commitment and tenacity to the path are unmistakable. Any accomplishment I have achieved, or credit given to our church, has not been done outside of her capable stride and ineffable leadership gift.

The Bible says that the way is narrow that leads to life. I know personally that the road to eternity is full of bends and curves that need to be navigated with wisdom and finesse. This book documents the journey. It invites you onto the pathway and compels you to keep your eyes on the destination. Bobbie's ability to allow the Spirit of God to speak to her, and then the grace with which she gives voice to His heart, will buoy your spirit. Her ability to discern where Christ is leading, to read the faces of her fellow sojourners, and spend her traveling time wisely sets her apart to speak of the longevity that we have enjoyed. When we embarked on the journey together, I knew she was meant to be my companion on the path—but I never anticipated the capacity, depth, and partnership that would grow within and for that I am immensely proud.

There is no one that I could recommend more highly. Within these pages she will quickly gain your trust as a shepherd and a friend, and I know her revelation and wisdom will encourage you to *stay the path* for the length of your days.

Brian Houston
Founder and global senior pastor of Hillsong Church
Bestselling author of Live, Love, Lead

STAY *the* PATH

ONE

IF MY JOURNEY COULD TEACH YOU ANYTHING

(An Introduction)

Y*ou haven't seen anything yet, woman of God. I don't know what you do, my sister, but I sense that you are in ministry.*" Her hot breath on my face startled me, and her words caused a gasp to ripple through the crowd.

Blank page, full heart, and a lifetime of experience—where do I begin to articulate with precision what has been of *defining revelation* to me personally, in order that it will be of interest and defining revelation to you? What could I possibly say that will resonate with your world and add to your well-being and success? I'm sure every writer, leader, or creative soul with similar "blank-page" and uncharted opportunity has felt the same.

Legacy is a noble concept. In essence it's about leaving a story of insight and wisdom for others—for those you deeply love (such as friends, family, and children) and for those who look to you for example, leadership, and influence. Therefore (chin cupped in hand, elbow on desk, and eyes gazing heavenward), at the risk of talking to myself in order to talk with you, what convictions have shaped my journey and kept it fiercely real? What pivotal moments have kept me on course when territory, terrain, and enemies have proven challenging? What prevailing grace has watered the love affair of my life and never failed—and what timeless truths have kept me sure-footed and secure on a path that is both unique and yet not uncommon to all?

TRUE FROM START TO FINISH

I guess if I were author and pastor Rick Warren, I would begin with "It all starts with God, and it's not about you," a world-famous statement from what has become a world-famous book. If I were the one who penned the book of Genesis, I would begin with the most definitive statement ever committed to paper: "In the beginning, *God*." And if I were the beloved Apostle who wrote the Gospel of John, I would begin with "In the beginning was the Word and the Word was with God, and the Word was God."

Eugene Peterson in the Message paraphrase frames this same gospel introduction like this:

Everything was created through him; nothing—not one thing!—came into being without him. What came into existence was Life, and the Life was *Light to live by*. The Life-Light blazed out of the darkness; the darkness couldn't put it out... The Word became flesh and blood, and moved into the neighborhood. We saw the glory with our own eyes, the one-of-a-kind glory, like Father, like Son, Generous inside and out, *true from start to finish*. (John 1:3–5, 14 MSG; emphasis mine)

True from start to finish. True from beginning to end. Life that was (and is) light to live by. Now there's a brilliant place to begin, and a brilliant reality worth aspiring to. Imagine having such words spoken of *your* life. Imagine it being said of you—*they lived true from start to finish*! They discerned the mystery of life and lived true to who they were. They discovered the unique reason of their existence and lived true to their *distinctive passage* through time and history.

The reality of life, dear friend, is both profound and yet simple. Everything "under the sun" (see Eccles. 1:9 NIV) has beginning and end, start and finish. Everything has a source of (true) origin with the intent of (true) purpose, completion, and fulfillment—yet it is what happens in between, along that journey from beginning to finish line, that is of paramount importance. I heard it said that the "dash" (or line) between a person's birth date and passing date is vitally important because it reveals both the reality and measure of that life. As grand and romantic as "purpose" and "destiny" sound—neither are *destinations* guaranteed with the blast of the starting gun or that first step out into the unknown adventure of what lies ahead. It's what happens thereafter that truly matters—and anyone with any degree of longevity to humbly boast of will agree.

I am neither Pastor Rick Warren (surprise, surprise) nor one of the original and ancient Apostles who recorded the timeless Word of God that has shaped humankind down through the ages. However, I am a trustworthy friend present in our here and now, seeking to be obedient and helpful with the writing of this book.

My hope is to lay out, with simplicity and relatable warmth, some of the markers of wisdom and experience that have shaped my life as a woman in leadership alongside my husband, Brian, and within the now many-layered story of Hillsong. I don't pretend to have life completely figured out, but I do have some distance that can be drawn upon—distance that now includes thousands of people around the world and that runs several generations deep.

In the book of Ecclesiastes, Solomon (the privileged son of psalmist King David) has a life-changing epiphany. Like many a human soul, he questions life and for a moment has a mini meltdown, vacillating between wisdom and despondency. Regardless of fame, fortune, and insane creative talent, it all pales into apparent nothingness for him, because without a sense of *true reason and true direction* it feels shallow and futile. For ten chapters Solomon ponders, pontificates, and agonizes, until wisdom prevails and trumps the despondency. He then makes several remarkable statements—one being that "the writing of many books is endless," and that if we are not careful, the study of too many words outside of the words of the one true Shepherd will merely produce weariness of body and soul (see Eccles. 12 AMP).

That little verse in the Old Testament is a personal measuring rod for me as I find myself in this new season of writing. My only desire with this book you hold in your hands is to give worthy expression to the goodness of the one true Shepherd who has journeyed with me through life and landscape, and who wishes to do the same for you. As Psalm 23 teaches, He is the Good Shepherd who leads and guides, prods and protects, as we travel with him from what is beginning to end. The mere fact that God is called Alpha and Omega, Beginning and End, is a rather brilliant clue that He knows what is best and most advantageous for all of us.

This remarkable Shepherd King teaches us how to handle the challenges and face the enemies. His words have the capacity to help us discern prevailing conditions and frame the seasons of life with wisdom. They show us how to rest and find ease, and yet also how to contend and war for what is noble and upright. It is the words of Christ that make us great, and it is His wisdom that secures our passage through life . . . and it is "safe passage through life" that endlessly defines my own passion (and maternal heart) as a pastor and shepherd within His church and kingdom.

MY HEART AND PRAYER

For those unfamiliar with my voice, I have been a Christ follower for more than forty years and a lover of the Lord Jesus since the moment He knocked on the door of my heart at fifteen. I have three adult children, each married to a fabulous partner, and at the time of penning this, we have seven cute grandbabies. I've had the magnificent honor of being in ministry alongside my husband, Brian, for over four decades, and in that time (pastoring an expansive global church) we've navigated some insane, crazy, scary, and wonderful territory together. My simple desire for this book, *Stay the Path*, is to share some of the truths that have kept us on course, on point, and focused on the path before us.

So this book comes to you with much love, heart, and affection.

My prayer is that if my journey has taught me anything, it may also teach and add to your experience. The Bible says that there is nothing new under the sun, but each and every day there are lessons to be learned and new applications of truth to be made. It's the voices of past, present, and future that teach us. The ancients of long ago have certainly left their legacy to glean from—and of course, the prophetic voices of old (that reach into and salt the future) are timeless. They echo into our here and now, and they draw us onward. Yet there are also many trustworthy voices alongside us now with perspective and experience worth listening to.

So as I launch out with "blank page, full heart," I am reminded of a milestone moment twenty years ago, a milestone moment that I repeatedly woke with in the dawn hours leading into beginning this book, and a moment that I believe the Spirit of God strategically brought back into view from the late nineties.

A MILESTONE MOMENT

It had been a full and busy day. In that season, I was navigating a young teenage family, a vibrant and rapidly expanding church, a lovely (yet crazy) visionary husband, and the very first aspects of a "God-whisper" that would become an all-consuming passion to this very day. (The God-whisper story is within my book *The Sisterhood*.)

For some reason, circumstances that day had been against me attending what was a retreat not far from where we lived on the outskirts of Sydney. However, that afternoon those circumstances changed. I organized my kids, and I found myself with a girlfriend racing out into the countryside to the campsite setting of this small but important conference. Not wanting to be a distraction, my friend and I quietly slipped into the meeting of not more than two hundred women and sat a few rows back from the front.

I can't recall many details of the night, except the fact that I probably should have been on the front row supporting this retreat, because my husband was "State Leader" of this denominational movement at the time. That aside, the invited guest speaker decided to pray for all the key leaders at the end of her message. With others, I walked to the front and stood (almost in the shadows) at the far end to the right.

As I closed my eyes in prayer, the speaker was at the complete other end. A lengthy row of fabulous women separated us, and if this woman intended to pray for each of us individually, then I would have been the last one she would have gotten to. As my heart leaned heavenward, I suddenly felt hot breath on my face. "The woman" was suddenly in front of me. Hot breath. For a split second I was confused. But before I had time to process another thought, she was declaring these exact and powerful words over my life: "You haven't seen anything yet, woman of God. I don't know what you do, my sister, but I sense that you are in ministry."

A gasp rippled through the audience. She was correct. I *was* in ministry. Brian and I led the state movement, and our Hillsong church had for some reason become the fastest growing in the nation. In the months ahead, when I was still happy to remain in the shadows, Brian would be elected as national president of that same movement. It was obvious this woman ministering had no idea of our role or influence, hence the murmur and sudden intrigue of what was about to be spoken over my life.

With uncanny prophetic clarity, authority, and emotion she began to declare words that I have never forgotten, words that framed the very heartbeat and core of our ministry, words that carried truth then, and even more so twenty years on: "**I heard the Lord say that you have plowed up hard ground, you've paved the way. Many have come along, and they have taken away pieces of the thing that you labored over, you worked over, you sought over, you cried over, you prayed over, the very thing that you birthed, and when you saw them come and take pieces away, you said, 'I bless them with it, Lord. They don't take anything. I give it to them, I give it to them.' And because you have, the anointing that is in the house has gone around the world, but you and the man of God have not yet seen anything.**"

My heart and mind were reeling. She continued, "**The Lord says, 'Daughter, you have built and built again and built again, but go home and tell the man of God, you are going to build again. You are going to build again. You made room for two thousand and then you made room for five thousand, but I said there needs to be room for twelve thousand,' says the Lord. Twelve thousand, for they will come from around the world to see the glory that is in the house.**

"**I have made your husband a man of truth. He loves truth at whatever the cost, and people either love him for it or they get mad at him for it, but he will not settle for anything less than truth, and because of his love for truth, I have allowed him to go to the next level of my anointing and my grace and my glory.**

"**Write the book, woman of God, write the book, write the book, write the book, write the book—make a recording of what you have birthed in the house so that it will be a training** manual for those who have lost their hope. Write the book, woman of God, and your children, it shall be a memorial for them to follow. For children, children, children shall know your God and they shall not follow the voice of a stranger and they will not know rebellion, but they will know My grace, My glory, My word, My song..."

And then the voice of this preacher woman broke with emotion—it was as though you could hear the affection of the Father in her words: "My song, My song, My song is in your house, My *song* is in your house. You built my house, now I'm going to build your house. You built my house, I'm going to build your house, and I will settle over it, and it won't just be something that you settle for, but it will be grander than what you've even desired. So I say, woman of God, thou hast done well with my anointing."

Okay. Personal words and personal promises are exactly that—they're personal. However, these words spoken on a tranquil evening in April 1997, in the rolling green countryside of northern Sydney, have affected not only my life but many others also. My prayer is that by the time we get to the closing chapters of this book, they will have shaped your world in some way also. They're words that have influenced not only our own natural children but also the many "spiritual children" within our church and ministry—including those who have poured through our leadership conferences and college over the years. As we have collectively leant into and experienced His grace, glory, word, and song, many have gone on to salt the Body of Christ around the world as a new breed of kingdom builders. The "song" she spoke of has become the arrowhead of a greater message about the cause of Christ and His passion for people, with our worship and music ministering to millions.

My husband has proven to be "a man of truth"—and as prophesied, some have hated him for it but multitudes have loved him for it. And if I can say this with humility of heart, our ministry has "paved a way" and cut a path for others to follow. The hard ground plowed has created a slipstream within the broad and diverse Body of Christ, allowing many to fast-track themselves into God's purpose and blessing for their lives.

The remarkable thing about those unexpected words of encouragement that evening was that, in the car driving to that campsite, I had been telling my friend how I had written my first book (*I'll Have What She's Having*) and had put it in a drawer nine months earlier because I felt awkward about it. Who was I to write a book? What did I have to bring to the table? How embarrassing! And then, an hour or so later, I'm standing on an altar with a wild and yet endearing woman who is declaring (with hot breath) that I should write the book that I had actually hidden away because of lack of confidence.

So as I begin, I share these words from 1997 because one of the mandates upon this little heart of mine is to "make a recording of what has been birthed in the house" in order that it become (as the woman prophesied) a memorial for others to follow and a training manual for those who have lost hope. I have no personal ambition outside of this, and I certainly know that I am not the only voice speaking to this current generation. My only desire is to be true to what Jesus has allowed me to be a part of and, with openhandedness, to offer any wisdom gained. After all, those words did say that as we have lived with open hand and generous heart, the anointing upon the house has gone out and around the world and influenced the way many approach modern-day Christianity and church.

COSTLY EXPERIENCE

So despite still feeling like a twenty-year-old in my head, my prayer is that the costly experience of my little sixty-year journey (thus far) will provide comfort, courage, and hope for others. I know you will agree that we each have only one life and it passes like a vapor. So, dear one—*if my journey could teach you anything*—if my life could add anything to yours, if my story can help you "stay the path" and fulfill all that is upon your life and eternal destiny, then the following pages hold a portion of what I would say to you.

I pray that you will hear the heart of God within my words, because as Solomon declared, "There is no end to the writing of books" (see Eccles. 12:12 NIV; paraphrase mine). None of us have time for human wisdom only. We all need divine wisdom, which issues from above and is perfect in every circumstance and season of life, enabling good success across the entire spectrum of our lives. As the psalmist says in Proverbs:

> My son [or daughter], be attentive to my wisdom [godly wisdom learned by *actual and costly experience*], and incline your ear to my understanding [of what is becoming and prudent for you], that you may exercise proper discrimination and discretion and your lips may guard and keep knowledge and the wise answer [to temptation]. (Proverbs 5:1 AMP; paraphrase and emphasis mine)

The destination is too precious to be compromised, so turn the page with me and allow a little lady from a land Down Under in Australia to share elements of what "the path" has taught her thus far. As we begin, allow me to pray for you.

"Father, thank you for the one holding this book, and that our lives are colliding within these pages. May the stories and words shared instill strength, hope, and endless courage. Thank you for this fabulous adventure called Life, thank you that we are not alone, that we are here to encourage and cheer one another on. Draw near, dear Holy Spirit, enable, teach, and equip us for all that lies ahead. Travel with us, Lord. We humbly commit our path and way to you. Amen."

TWO

STAY HOMEWARD BOUND
(Compelled)

I t's okay, darling...if we die...we will go to heaven...[*awk-ward pause*]...It's just getting there."

His words were designed to instill peace and confidence into his brand-new bride of two days—a new bride who now stood ankle-deep in ocean water, drenched to the bone and marginally white with shock.

Our wedding had been gorgeous. We tied the knot on a balmy summer evening in New Zealand. I walked down the aisle of the little A-frame church, wearing a lace tiered dress with pastel silk flowers meticulously embroidered by my ever-devoted and talented mother. He wore a pale blue suit (aptly and strangely called the "Houston") with tan-colored shoes. With flowers in my hair, we exchanged vows that we can still recite to this day—and our Scottish friend Marilyn sang a song that boasted the line "eternally grateful" over and over. We were young, naive, and madly in love. When Brian proposed—although I'm not sure he actually did propose properly, because I think we just assumed that we would get married—he said, "Bobbie, I need you to know that we may never own a home or have anything of substance to our name." Those things honestly didn't matter. We were in love with each other, and in love with a sense of calling to serve and give all for the kingdom of God.

On the third night of our honeymoon, we slept on Brian's parents' lounge-room floor (in Wellington), before borrowing his mum's little blue Ford Escort for an exotic (smile) honeymoon around the South Island of New Zealand—staying in "camping ground cabins" and bunking down with any random friends who would accommodate us. As we drove and parked the little blue Escort in the lower regions of the inter-island ferry (that connected the North and South Islands of New Zealand), we had no idea what awaited us. Our marriage had just begun. Our destiny together had just begun. What could possibly assail such a perfect adventure so newly set in motion?

We settled into our front-row seats in the (front) lounge, which seated around one hundred people. The inter-island ferry wasn't a little tugboat affair. She was a decent-size ship with cars beneath, several lounges and bars, and even room for the train that connected the two main islands of the country. This lounge felt like the equivalent of being on the third or fourth story of a tall building. All that lay before us was the bow of the ship, a stretch of ocean, and the wonder of a road trip around the glorious South Island of our homeland—mountains, lakes, New Zealand's famous "hokey pokey" honeycomb ice cream, and enough green pasture to accommodate the sixty million sheep the country boasted of back in the day.

An older gentleman sat across the aisle from us. As everyone got settled, I recall him standing in front of the giant windows, showing his little grandson the sights to be seen. As we excitedly headed out of the harbor and into open waters, the conditions suddenly changed. These waters were notorious for flaring up and had tragically claimed fifty-three lives when another ship (the *Wahine*) had foundered in 1968. Despite being only yards from shore, the ship lay on her side, being lashed by wind and waves, with the rescue mission unable to save those who were perishing.

I'd grown up fishing with my dad, and although we only ever fished in a humble little "tinny" (Aus/NZ term for a lightweight aluminum boat), he had taught me a healthy respect of the ocean. As the inter-island ferry headed toward her destination, the front-row ride in the front lounge began to feel more like a roller-coaster ride. At first it was fun and a little bit exciting— and then my demeanor changed. I felt my body tense as we found ourselves looking up at walls of green water. I exaggerate not. The ocean conditions had turned, and now this ship was plowing through giant waves. The bow of the boat would take the power of the wave—water and spray filling the air. With every crash, a ripple of reaction could be heard across the lounge and I would shut my eyes with the impact. The old gentleman and his grandson took their seats (across the aisle from us), because the ride was making it difficult to stand.

Suddenly another giant wave emerged, but this time from the side. There was no way the bow of the ship was going to break its impact. Almost in slow motion it rose from the ominous sea and crashed against the front of the ship, the deck, and the front lounge windows. Again, I instinctively closed my eyes. And then, like in a bad dream, the wall of water crashed through the windows and across the entire lounge. All I recall in the moment is the realization that the ocean was inside the boat.

Brian and I opened our eyes. Everyone was drenched. People were screaming. Blood was flowing because glass from the window had shattered and swept across the passengers. I had glass all through my long dark hair and inside my clothes. I heard that a man was in the bathroom at the rear of this lounge when suddenly water came over the cubicle wall! Let me elaborate: A man is in a ship, in a lounge, in the men's bathroom—and inside a cubicle. Can you imagine what went through his mind when a wall of water came over the door!?

Brian glanced at the old gentleman across the aisle. Part of the window frame was literally twisted around his neck. "I think we need to move," Brian said. The reality was that we didn't know what was coming next—another wave or worse.

The old man was miraculously okay. The crew told us that if they had closed the shutters on the windows, he probably would have been decapitated. I bent down for my handbag (women do strange things in moments of crisis) but it had been completely washed away. We moved toward the rear of the lounge. As the ship's crew tried to bandage and calm people, as we stood in the receding water, and as the captain tried to steady the ship, my dear husband spoke the words I opened this chapter with: "It's okay, darling... if we die... we go to heaven... *It's just getting there.*"

LIFE IS A PILGRIMAGE

Life is indeed a journey and pilgrimage. As stated already, it has a critical starting point and a critical finish line—and the finish line is heaven. *We are spiritual beings, on a spiritual journey, to a spiritual destination.* Those of atheist or agnostic persuasion may disagree, but just because you can't see or believe, that doesn't mean something can't or doesn't exist. There are many things within the realm of nature and universe that I personally can't see or fathom, yet my lack of comprehension doesn't negate their (felt) existence. It's the same with heaven. When faith is entered into and when the "eyes of your understanding" (Eph. 1:18 KJV) are opened, heaven becomes a compelling revelation and conviction. It is the eternal hope of every believer and follower of Christ, and it is the eternal compass that draws us onward and upward (see Eccles. 3:11 AMP). It is the conviction that keeps one homeward bound...so if my journey could teach you anything, I would compel you to seek and find the truth on this one. It is impossible to "stay the path" when you don't believe there is a path or a God who is fiercely committed to you.

In the (New Testament) book of Hebrews, the writer frames it so clearly:

Do you see what this means—all these pioneers *who blazed the way*, all these veterans cheering us on? It means we'd better get on with it. Strip down, start running—and *never quit!* No extra spiritual fat, no parasitic sins.

Keep your eyes on Jesus, who both *began and finished* this race we're in. Study how he did it. Because he never *lost sight* of where he was headed—that exhilarating finish in and with God—he could put up with anything along the way: cross, shame, whatever. And now he's there, in the place of honor, right alongside God. When you find yourselves *flagging* in your faith, go over that story again, item by item, that long litany of hostility he plowed through. That will shoot adrenaline into your souls!... God is *educating* you; that's why you must never drop out. He's treating you as dear children. This *trouble* you're in isn't punishment; it's training, the normal experience of children. Only irresponsible parents leave children to fend for themselves...But God is doing what is best for us, training us to live God's holy best. At the time, discipline isn't much fun. It always feels like it's going against the grain. Later, of course, it pays off handsomely, for it's the well-trained who *find themselves* mature in their relationship with God. So don't sit around on your hands! No more dragging your feet! *Clear the path* for long-distance runners so no one will trip and fall, so no one will step in a hole and sprain an ankle. Help each other out. And run for it! (Hebrews 12:1–3, 7–8, and 10–13 MSG; emphasis mine)

As I ponder Brian's words to me on that boat all those years ago, I am reminded of how true they were. He was merely try-ing to calm the growing fear he saw in my young face. Had we perished that day, we would have boldly and confidently entered heaven, because for each of us "salvation in Christ" was as real and sure as the air we were breathing, but the process would have been harrowing.

God's intent for all of us is safe passage. His heart is that "har-rowing" is a word not found in our vocabulary as we describe life, yet the prevailing reality of life is that we live in a fallen (and often harrowing) world. There is an enemy and there is a sin factor, with consequent fallout of human behavior. Passage is not always smooth. Passage is not always safe and sound, exempt of risk or challenge. Passage is sometimes strewn with everyone else's mess and dysfunction. Passage sometimes throws unexpected curveballs (or curve waves), and sometimes what comes at us can be as shocking and frightening as a wall of water over the bathroom cubicle door of an ocean liner.

I challenge you to stir up the revelation and conviction of who you are, where you are headed, and what you are about, because without such convictions you might find yourself easy prey for being thrown off course or swayed. The prevailing conviction of my life, as both a girl with heaven in her eyes and a minister of the gospel with a responsibility toward those entrusted to her, is that we all make it home to heaven. That single thought has become the "one thing" of my life. It honestly governs my responses and reactions as an individual, wife, mother, grandmother, and minister, and it is the one thing that has seriously kept me on course.

Of course, there have been times when I've felt like quitting—what honest person in life or leadership hasn't? For the record, I don't plan ever to quit on my love for Jesus. However, the realities, pressures, and challenges of life in the "kingdom lane," or the "I-want-to-change-the-world lane," or the lane that adheres to destiny, calling, and wonder, are real. The Bible is full of exhortation to avoid such temptation, but I love how the ancient writer of Hebrews puts it. In the verses above, those who have preceded us are described as pioneers who blazed the way. And therein lies some reassuring love and perspective for all of us. We are not alone. We are not the only ones who have ever experienced the complexity of life. We are, however, privileged to be twenty-first-century runners—the ones who have a plethora of wisdom and experience to draw from. These ancient trailblazers (and many others since) have gone ahead. They wait for us in heaven, and if we believe the words in Hebrews 12, they're cheering us on. So let's take heart in the human story we find ourselves within, and let's play our part.

THE HUMAN STORY IS TAPESTRY IN MOTION

So, dear friend, what *compels* you? You may or may not see yourself as a trailblazer, but we all get to blaze (or shape) the trail for someone—for those we share life with or for those we encounter along the way. What leaves you no choice? What causes you to get up in the morning and then retire at night, knowing that another day of potential hope and opportunity awaits you when you open those sweet, sleepy eyes? What energizes you? What comforts you? What makes you rise above your weakness and seek what is beyond your own strength? What causes you to persevere beyond the capacity that often feels lacking? What do you observe of life and people, and what is of importance to you? I'm not alluding to perfection here. I'm certainly not "Miss Perfect" with everything figured out (trust me). However, the conviction that all of humanity is homeward bound is a powerful conviction to live by. Homeward bound with a day of reckoning for all—a day of reckoning for both the righteous and the unrighteous, the right standing and the ill standing.

I have a friend. Her name is Margaret. She's possibly one of the most stoic and adorable people you will ever meet. I met her in Scotland—she was telling her testimony with a giant cigarette as a prop, which was both hilarious and (obviously) memorable. Her story is one of abuse and disappointment, yet somewhere in the mix of life she encountered truth that set her free. She's a tad older than me and she's the face you want to see in the crowd when you are speaking, because she's always sitting upright, with a smile on her dial and a stance that makes you think you are saying the most profound things ever spoken. She has recently retired as part of our Hillsong College faculty, where much of her role was to pastor (and mother) many of our students. She's a bright, intelligent, overcoming woman. One day I heard her say, "You know ... everyone goes to heaven ... but sadly, not everyone gets to *stay*."

I will never forget those words: "Not everyone gets to stay." They're not exactly lightweight in the punch they carry, yet, if you ponder them in light of the Word of God, they're true. All of humankind will one day stand before the Creator and God of the universe. Where and what that looks like is a mystery yet to be experienced, but the Bible makes abundantly clear that we will each give an account of our lives ... with consequences that will follow. Hopefully beautiful consequences, where we will hear words like "Well done, good and faithful servant ... Enter into the joy of your master" (Matt. 25:23 ESV), or words of love and embrace that welcome us home and usher us into a world beyond our wildest imagination. Hopefully we will hear shouts of joy and encouragement from those who have gone before, from those who have watched our progress and been part of the great host cheering us onward—yet Christ did not hide the fact that there will also be those who are tragically turned away. Turned away not because God is mean or unkind, but because life is a journey toward an eternity that has two destinations. Jesus came to create a divide in a road that was headed one way to destruction—a fork where salvation, rescue, and everlasting life is offered, and where humanity gets to make a choice in favor of life over death (see Deut. 30:19).

The reason I choose to "stay the path" is because, unashamedly, I want to make it to heaven. I'm homesick for this eternal and celestial city that has captivated mankind's imagination since the beginning of time. I love the Lord Jesus Christ, I recognize the great price He paid for my personal salvation, and I don't want to make His sacrifice null and void by failing to lean into all He has done. And I choose to stay the path because I honestly angst at the thought of people being turned away— of people forfeiting their beautifully "prepared place" in heaven (see John 14) because they lost sight of the prize, got weary of it all, or failed to appropriate His divine enablement for the journey. I am aware that I have a part to play in His great salvation plan, as do you, dear friend. The Great Commission (belonging to all of us) is to stand in that fork and be willing to point the correct way to those willing to be directed. The Great Commission is about our lives being a clear signpost home.

The human story involves us all. It's a pilgrimage of a million interwoven stories. In fact, if this planet currently boasts over seven billion inhabitants, that means there are over seven billion stories in play: Seven billion pathways leading somewhere; seven billion pathways converging where people can either engage or disengage with truth; seven billion beautiful souls within this generation alone who are going to hear "Welcome home, beloved" or "Beloved, I'm sorry but I never knew you" (see Matt. 7:21–23).

This may sound intense, but friend, our lives are not merely our own. We belong to a much greater eternal landscape that is in motion whether we fully understand it or not. I chose this path when I was fifteen, clueless of all it represented. All I knew was that Jesus was suddenly more real than life itself, and I wanted this God who had arrested my attention and heart. Forty-five years later, at age sixty, I still choose this path, because the conviction hasn't changed. In fact, it's more compelling than ever.

HOMECOMING IS NOT A COMPETITION

The Gospel of John records the most beautiful words ever spoken by Jesus. They are words that continually compel my heart with hope and anticipation:

> "Let not your hearts be *troubled*. Believe in God; believe also in me. In my Father's house are many rooms. If it were not so, would I have told you that I go to prepare a place for you? And if I go and prepare a place for you, I will *come again* and will take you to myself, that where I am you may be also. And you know *the way* to where I am going." Thomas said to him, "Lord, we do not know where you are going. How can we know the way?" Jesus said to him, "*I am the way, and the truth, and the life.* No one comes to the Father except through me. If you had known me, you would have known my Father also. From now on you do know him and *have seen him.*" (John 14:1–7 ESV; emphasis mine)

This pathway home is neither a competition nor a race. It's the road that all mankind walks—from Adam and Eve to you and I here now within these pages. No one is competing for your

personal reward—fought for, won, and made available through
Christ. The reward is yours. It has your name upon it, as does
the glorious address and place prepared for you. Homecoming belongs to all of us. None of my natural children have to
compete with one another to come home to our family house.
Perhaps the great eternal sadness (despite the immense joy
promised) will be rooms and mansions never occupied because
people failed to choose correctly. I hope I am wrong, but nevertheless there is nothing more sad than a family sitting down
to Christmas or Thanksgiving dinner with empty places at the
table because dysfunction, tragedy, or failure to engage has prevented them from being filled. An invitation exists to the greatest celebration ever—it's just a case of whether people respond
or not.

It is imperative that this core conviction compel us, and that
is my prayer for you as I share some of the bends and curves,
highs and lows, challenges and enemies that we have faced and
that (as already stated) are not uncommon for any one of us.
Turn the page and I might jump straight into the battlescape.

By the way, we survived the ocean experience on our honeymoon. The captain, who had years of experience, read the
prevailing conditions, steadied the boat, and brought us safely
to shore. I may have thrown up (sorry), and I may have slept
the entire way around the South Island (post-shock reaction and
lingering motion sickness), but we lived to tell the story. If you
offered me a holiday on a cruise ship, I'd probably decline (still
wounded), but I've learned lessons from the ordeal—mainly that
my captain, Jesus, is with us in every storm and crisis. I know
that sounds a bit cliché, but it's true. I learned three days into
our marriage that Christ is in the midst of every turbulence life

may throw at you. This God I speak of will never leave or forsake you. So take heart if that's what you need to hear personally. Flip the page and allow me to take you into one of the most daunting days in my life, a day that began a series of battles that lasted many years, but which has instilled a steely fortitude and resolve that I would not exchange for anything.

THREE

STAY WITHIN THE BATTLESCAPE

(The Frontline)

The Life-Light blazed out of the darkness (and) the darkness couldn't put it out.

JOHN 1:5 MSG; PARENTHESES AND

EMPHASIS MINE

Darkness is defined as both the absence of light and the inherent lack of spiritual enlightenment. It has within its context unhappiness, distress, and gloom—it also includes forces described as wicked and evil. The word "battle" is found within the meaning of war, which is defined as hostility or armed conflict between different nations, states, or groups. The accompanying synonyms of "bloodshed," "warfare," "combat," and "struggle" describe a world of relativity within what can present as the "battlescape" of our lives.

Sometimes in our first-world reality we joke that "the struggle is real." That could mean anything from a broken fingernail (ladies) to a slow Internet connection, an irritating few pounds that won't shift on the scales (a universal conspiracy) to that favorite dish that has (alas) run out at our favorite eating hole. The struggle is so real, right? Don't feel condemned. I think we all whine at times over things that don't really matter on the scale of eternity, and then arrest ourselves and say, "Yeah, sorry, first-world problems."

What family boasting offspring hasn't had to separate combating kids or teenagers, who can contend over the most trivial of things. My boys are great mates, but when they were growing up, there were those occasional moments when they came, contending and combative, to their mother. I had no time to peace-negotiate (sorry, bad confession—working mom), especially when it was a case of "he said, she said" (although they were both boys)—who can successfully mediate that argument without a law degree? So I would send them to their rooms and tell them to figure it out themselves. Possibly not the best parenting advice, but they usually did work it out and we're all here today with a healthy respect for one another. Sometimes when you give the mindless contentions no audience, you diffuse the power of what is trying to divide—although, having said that, I think you would want to know that there is enough God-deposit within your kids to peace-make the situation rather than kill each other.

On a more sobering note, my father, Arthur Gordon

McDonald, entered the battlescape of the Second World War in
the late 1930s. That *battle*, whose consequent bloodshed claimed
sixty million lives, was for the freedom of the then world, including the demise of a certain madman hell-bent on the genocide of
an entire people. I possess a tiny faded picture of my father's regi-
ment marching to their ship in New Zealand. A long sea journey
awaited them as they headed toward the Middle East. Alongside
my father and his ANZAC mates (the Australian and New Zealand Army Corps), the image captures a young bride of three
weeks (my mother) and her girlfriend (my auntie Olive) running
beside them on the road. The image portrays the romance and
weightiness of all lovers separated at poignant times of war and
deployment.

This world is awash with battles of all kinds.

Someone contending for peace within a fractured marriage
may feel like they are in the battle of their lives. Someone facing
a losing battle against an incurable disease may feel completely
overwhelmed and defeated within the trenches, and someone
who has lost a child or loved one may feel, in their deep sorrow,
like there is no reason to get up again and press on. Right now,
as a global community, we have an unprecedented humanitarian crisis happening on our watch because of war and mankind's
inability (outside of Christ) to cohabit peaceably. It seems that
Jesus' warnings of "wars and rumors of wars" (Matt. 24:6) are at
an all-time high. Some debate that the world has always been
like this—the only difference being that the media now brings
it to harsh reality within our own living rooms—but personally,
I'm not so sure. I believe we are living in what the Bible calls the
"latter days," and what we are experiencing are the "birth pangs"
of the end.

A FRACTURED DAY

The battlescape and toll of conflict within everyday life look different for all of us, but one battlescape is common to all—and that's the *spiritual battle* that the Bible is so clear about. It's the spiritual battle between light and darkness, good and evil, and it is the divine plan of heaven above to restore humanity to the full intent of God's heart and goodness. It's the battle against an enemy that is fiercely opposed to you living in your God-given potential and taking the ground that God has purposed for you to take. It's the battle against an enemy that loathes the Church of Jesus Christ advancing on the earth and taking territory that the instigator of this darkness thinks is his. It's the battle that Jesus spoke of and warned of, and it's the same big-picture battle that earlier generations experienced. When the goodness of God begins to take *influential shape* on the earth, trust me, all hell reacts to compromise, discredit, sabotage, and destroy. It's the battle that the twenty-first-century maturing church has to be aware of, not in a weird and woeful way, but in a way that simply recognizes what is going on and presses on regardless.

It was in such a spiritual battlescape that I found myself one Friday afternoon in the late nineties—a day that felt calm in the natural, yet time has proven that something dark was brewing to assault and fracture all that is precious to God. If my journey is to teach you anything, I must share some of the lessons learned from this season, because tenacity and endurance in the face of the battle are critical if we are to stay the path.

My phone rang as I mingled with the girls.

It was just before midday, and I had just finished speaking at our Sisterhood women's meeting in our newly acquired city campus in downtown Sydney. I had spoken a message called "Kingdom Women Make Mincemeat of Their Enemies." I had been camped within the Proverbs 31 woman for a period of time, and I was up to a verse that spoke of this godly woman arising while it was yet night (implying adversity) and getting food for her family. I felt the verse spoke to more than simply being a good and studious housewife. It was speaking to the warrior-like fighting spirit that I know resides within every woman. I married the message with Psalm 23, where the psalmist speaks of God preparing a table before us in the presence of our enemies— suggesting that in life there are enemies who surface from time to time with the intent to harass, steal, kill, and ultimately destroy, but God is able to prepare a table (of grace, provision, and weapons of warfare) between us and them.

It was a memorable message, and the buzz after our gathering could be felt. It was in this context that my phone rang. It was Brian. I recall him saying, "I need to take you to lunch." Okay, what wife doesn't love that? But he knew that I was in the city and he knew that I normally took a handful of girls out for lunch each Friday. "But darling, I'm planning to go to lunch with—" He interrupted and pressed the point: "I *need* to take you to lunch."

We met in a restaurant on the edge of the harbor. As I recall, it was a beautiful day and everything seemed perfect—Sydney's inner-city skyline looked gorgeous against the blue sky, and I felt good because I'd delivered the message that was burning in my heart and that I had labored over all week. As we sat in the open-air café, Brian dropped the news about the day that he himself describes as the worst day of his life. It related to his father and newly surfaced accusations of child abuse (by his father) that had occurred thirty years earlier.

I don't feel led to explain the details of his father's deep failings (you can read them yourself in Brian's book *Live Love Lead*), but as my husband shared what was so heavy upon his heart, I felt my own heart sink to the floor. In those blinding moments of shock and horror, of trying to process the heart-wrenching, disturbing words, I remember thinking, "I need to listen to my own message again"—the message I had just preached an hour or so earlier. A message that had tried to show the girls what to do when unexpected news comes and your world is assailed by something too difficult to digest or bear. A message that challenged those present to believe that nothing is beyond God's grace and ability to redeem. A message that reminded us all that whatever brokenness, pain, or tragedy has happened, God is able to intervene—and that if all hell confronts you, the promise of the Good Shepherd (Psalm 23) is that He is able to prepare a table before you in the presence of those enemies. A message that, should we take a leaf from the Proverbs 31 woman, teaches that we can rise in the midst of adversity (deep, dark adversity) and turn any mess, tragedy, and horror into a spiritual meal or a message that can and will help others.

That lunchtime date with my husband marked the beginning of what has possibly been the greatest battlescape within our personal lives and the life of our church. Again, it is something Brian writes of within his book—but as "Mrs. *Live Love Lead*" I want to share truths learned from that landscape. As the woman who has been alongside her man for forty years now, as a woman who has stood in the gap when he was too weakened to stand, and as a woman who has a revelation that we are created with strengths perfect for battle and endurance, I want to turn what the enemy has meant for evil (against us personally) into something that will encourage you as it did me. Therefore, dear friend, if my journey could teach you anything from the frontline trenches of what I affectionately see as the battlescape of Christ's glorious passion and Great Commission, I would say:

NO WEAPON FORMED AGAINST YOU SHALL PROSPER

As I begin to give you a handful of thoughts, I would say, first and foremost, that the perfect, timeless, and infallible Word of God, quickened and engrafted within you (personally), and then tested and tried in you (personally), is what will engraft you personally into an unshakable kingdom.

While we glean from others and those who have gone before, God does not have grandchildren, only children. That is why every person who professes Christ as Lord is going to experience situations somewhere in their journey that are designed to make them sit up, rise up, and mature in stature. It's the rise-up moments that *solidify our faith and steel the convictions of our heart.* It's the rise-up moments that sort the men from the boys, and often position you differently on the front lines of life, ministry, and "Thy kingdom come."

Not every drama that happens in life can be blamed on the forces of darkness. If someone has abused their health all their life and then falls prey to ill health, more than likely they can't blame the devil for their troubles. Across many aspects of life, the enemy can take advantage of a door left open or exposed, but there are many things within our existence that are not the work of sinister forces. Sometimes the enemy does set bad choices before us, and then once the bait (or temptation) is taken, he pretty much leaves us alone to track ourselves down our own path of destruction.

I'm not addressing those kinds of realities (which, by the way, can be overcome and restored through new right choices and the grace of our good, good God)—what I'm talking about here are *real spiritual weapons* that are formed against us, with intent to hurt the advancement of God's kingdom in and through us. Let me camp for a moment in Hebrews and Isaiah. Hebrews 12 tells us that everything on Earth that can be shaken will be shaken, but it also tells us that we have not come to a fragile kingdom that can be easily swayed—rather, we have come to *an unshakable kingdom in Christ*:

> *But you* have come to Mount Zion and to the city of the living God, the heavenly Jerusalem, and to *innumerable angels* in festal gathering, and to the *assembly* of the firstborn who are enrolled in heaven, *and to God*, the judge of all, and to the spirits of the righteous made perfect, and to *Jesus*, the mediator of a new covenant . . . Therefore let us be grateful for receiving a kingdom that *cannot be shaken*, and thus let us offer to God acceptable worship, with reverence and awe, for *our God is a consuming fire*. (Hebrews 12:22–24 and 28–29 ESV; emphasis mine)

As Christ followers, we are already on the "front foot" in any spiritual battle because of the truth within these verses. Isaiah 54 then goes on (prophetically) to frame a number of realities that are the promise to those whose life is hid in Him. It speaks of barrenness not being a problem to God—which is good news because one of the major strategies against legacy is barrenness, which can present in several ways. It strongly exhorts that if we sing and rejoice and continue to press onward (enlarging and stretching, despite the challenges), we will experience generational blessing beyond our wildest imagination. It declares that if we continue to endure, the promise will enable our children to inhabit the earth and turn the desolate places of humanity into places of blessing:

> *Enlarge* the place of your tent, and let the curtains of your habitations be stretched out; do not hold back; lengthen your cords and strengthen your stakes. For you will *spread abroad* to the right and to the left, and your *offspring will possess the nations* and will people the desolate cities. (Isaiah 54:2–3 ESV; emphasis mine)

Fabulous promises. And then the verses that aren't quite as enthralling—verses that make it quite clear that these promises will also inspire opposition. It warns that voices of accusation, and weapons to discredit and harm, will rise up against us, but they shall not prosper:

> *No weapon* that is fashioned against you shall succeed, and you shall refute every tongue that rises against you in judgment. This is the heritage of the servants of the LORD and *the vindication from me*, declares the LORD. (Isaiah 54:17 ESV; emphasis mine)

Isaiah 54 was the foundational chapter that stirred Brian's parents before they decided to come to Sydney in 1977 to pioneer Christian Life Center. We arrived six months later and joined that congregation before leaving in 1983 to pioneer our own church, Hillsong. Amid these verses and an all-night stirring vision of "wheat fields blowing in the wind, that then turned to oceans and oceans and oceans of worshipping hands" are verses that also speak of weapons being forged against this expansive promise.

I am very aware that my husband and I (together with our Hillsong Church) are living in the promise of Isaiah 54. We are a church and ministry witnessing latter-day harvest fields— oceans of souls turning to Jesus every week and worshipping like there is no tomorrow. God has allowed us, as a church, to enter spiritually desolate cities and places hardened to the gospel, and see miraculous breakthroughs. We are a church with a very strong generational testimony. The promise that the "offspring" of the house will spread abroad to the east and west, and the global description of our church as "one house with many rooms," are literally true, with many agreeing that a unique anointing resides upon us to plant and pioneer churches around the world. In our homeland of Australia, God has blessed us with uncanny favor— favor that often has secular Australia bewildered. It's favor that the real enemy (the devil) hates. If the enemy wants to marginalize (or minimize) the church in Australia, he often does so by aiming his arrows at us personally.

As a couple, family, and church, we've endured unreasonable attack for many, many years (most of it because of the fallout of Brian's father's sins), but the point I want to make is that, as you keep your heart clean, pure, and undaunted, as you live open, honest, and true to the one true judge (God), as you live dependent on His outpoured Spirit and mindful always that the Father is the one who vindicates, as you pray for those who persecute and despise you, and as you (very important) press on in the path before you . . . *no weapon formed against you shall ever prosper.*

The Father never promised that the "way home" would be easy. It isn't. Peel it back a layer and it's a vehement battlescape where life and death, heaven and hell, demons and angels struggle. It's a way carved forward only because Jesus allowed himself to be the sacrifice for our redemption. But the prevailing perspective I want to bring to you today is that (again) no weapon formed against you shall prosper if you stay on the straight and narrow. So if my journey could teach you anything, dear one, it is this fact. I often joke that we are going to make it home to heaven one way or another—we might arrive scarred and marginally dragging ourselves over the line, but we are going to stay the course and fight to the end for the prize that is Jesus. May we echo the words of the Apostle Paul: "I have fought the *good fight*, I have finished the race, I have kept the faith" (2 Tim. 4:7 ESV; emphasis mine).

THE FRONT LINE COMES WITH TERRITORY

The front line definitely comes with territory. Get used to it. You can't aspire to be on the front line of influence, blessing, and wonder without realizing that it comes with certain pioneering territory. I think the thought is obvious, but nevertheless it's amazing how many people (and especially young people) want the favor of success and advancement and yet are shocked and rattled when they face a hint of opposition or realize the territory has a very real price tag attached.

Anyone who has advanced a dream of any kind in business or ministry has experienced this reality. So rather than fight the reality ("woe is me, life is unfair, I didn't sign up for this"), instead steel up and realize that if God has called you, then he has also graced you for whatever territory you encounter. In the Old Testament, the forefathers faced some giants on the way to the promised land, and in the same way, God is never going to require of us what we are unable to deliver or walk in. It sounds fabulous in theory, but again, it is outworked experientially in our lives, and it is what causes you to have voice, influence, and credibility that will make others want to follow.

Our natural and spiritual family is blessed on so many levels, but (trust me) we have paid an enormous price for the favor entrusted. Yes, it is magnificent and wonderful (and to the uninformed or misinformed it could appear glamorous, which it isn't), yet let me repeat: It has come with a hefty price tag of hard work, devotion, and at times persecution. The only time I ever almost lost it and wanted to quit was when we suffered sustained and fierce media attack that included lies and nonsense about our children. For a split second I reasoned that my children did not ask for this. Attack Brian and me if you must, but don't touch my kids. For a split-second moment (where demons probably drooled in anticipation), I fell "out of love" with my nation. I suddenly did not like Australia, because it seemed like there was no justice to be found against the lies, innuendo, and hatred being leveled against us. But (Praise God) I entertained that thought only for a moment, because I recognized that that was indeed the strategy of the enemy. His plan was for me to fall out of love with a nation I deeply love. When you fall out of love with something, you suddenly don't care anymore. You no longer have the energy to labor for it, pray for it, lay your life down for it, or do whatever it takes for its welfare or future. I'm grateful that I had (spiritual) eyes to see and understand that day. Rather than quit, I chose godly resolve that made me "rise up" and continue to believe for an island continent that is my home and over which so many promises of revival have been spoken.

I don't know what you are facing, my friend. I've taken time over this thought because it deserves more than one or two paragraphs. My prayer is that you will sense the calling of God, and that no matter what the challenge is, you will rise up in the spirit of Isaiah 54 and "sing" to your God. Command your spirit to sing, rejoice, and hope. Look heavenward, take heart, and take godly authority over any strategy of the enemy pressing against you—and then, press on with determination to stay the path!

Your world may be vastly different from mine, but the bottom line is the same: When it comes to your life, God wants you to advance and repossess the desolate places of your own family, sphere, and world. You can do it. God is for us and not against us, and as Isaiah so beautifully scribes, *he is the God who vindicates*. Learn to love the front line for all her blessings and all her challenges. Remember always that it is a war we are in and that God is the one who vindicates when it seems there is nowhere else to turn. Arm yourself with all Christ has provided (that spectacular Ephesians 6 armor) and stand strong—stand strong for yourself, for your children (natural and spiritual), and for those God has destined you to influence.

Always remember:

Good strongholds will always trump bad strongholds. In Psalm 27:1 David says, "The LORD is my light and my salvation; whom shall I fear? The LORD is the *stronghold* of my life; of whom shall I be afraid?"

The book of Joel proclaims: "The LORD *roars* from Zion, and utters his voice from Jerusalem, and the heavens and the earth quake. But the LORD is a refuge to his people, a *stronghold* to the people of Israel" (Joel 3:16 ESV; emphasis mine).

And in 2 Corinthians 10:4 we have a trustworthy reminder: "For the weapons of our warfare are not of the flesh but have divine power to destroy *strongholds*" (ESV; emphasis mine).

Strongholds can be viewed in either the positive or negative. Many people attest that prior to salvation they had some not-so-brilliant strongholds shaping or controlling their lives— be that mind-sets, habits, or addictions—which is why we are exhorted to renew our thinking and submit to God's life-giving and freedom-rendering Word (see Rom. 8). The bottom line is that we can establish "wonderful strongholds" in our lives that are unshakable in the face of adversity.

We live in a world currently assaulted by terrorism. Strongholds of darkened ideology—that (by their obvious devastating effect) have been hatched in hell—are taking hold of people's minds with horrific outcome. We cannot live fearful, but we must ensure that the strongholds of our own lives are secure. Strongholds where we know (according to the Word of God) that love will always trump hatred and fear, and where kindness, acceptance, grace, and embrace will always disarm intolerance and prejudice. Strongholds where the Christlike response of forgiveness will always take the higher ground over offense or whatever else seeks to wound and destroy the human experience.

I want to encourage you that when you are in the trenches, you are making endless choices that are shaping the outcome of the battle. If you want to emerge triumphant and relatively unscathed by the experience, you have to make the "right choices"—continually. The battle is not optional. You can't sit there, hiding, hoping, and wishing it will all go away. You must act—and act swiftly—according to the Word. If I were talking to my kids, I would say, "Get it right and do it fast."

One of the strategies of the enemy on the spiritual battle-scape is to exhaust your proactive energies—to create diversions of worry and anxiety that consume your mind and drain your emotional energy. When I feel "the heat of the battle," I am quick these days to stop my spirit and mind from going down these side paths that do little except lead you into cycles of despair. Instead, speak to your soul realm. Remind yourself of who you are and whose you are. You belong to the fearsome and wonderful God whose name is Jehovah, Yahweh, Prince of Peace, King of kings, and Lord of lords—a God whose arm is not so short that it cannot save (Isaiah 59:1), a God who is moved with compassion toward His children and who identifies with the challenges of this present darkness. The Son of God became a man in order that He could rescue us. There is no temptation or challenge that Christ is unfamiliar with. Remind yourself of verses such as the ones I am quoting. Seek them out yourself and endlessly commit your way to Him. Trust in His divine care and keep pressing onward.

The face of the battle might be different, but the principles and lessons are the same. Our battles are not the same. You may never experience the battlefield that has been our experience. When our church surfaced a number of years ago above the radar of what the world perceives the church should be—*old, small, depleted, impoverished, insignificant, without creativity,*

color, excellence, innovation, or influence, and just plain boring—
we encountered a series of attacks designed to undermine and
discredit us. Marginal understatement there, but I don't want
to camp too much on the negative. Your battle might be completely different. It may involve health or family or something
else, but I am discovering that regardless of what the heat or
firing line looks like, what we all end up learning is essentially
the same.

We discover a God who never fails. We discover often that
there is more within us than we knew. It's amazing what adversity will reveal, and discovering that the God-deposit within you
is stronger than you realized is surprisingly wonderful. Sometimes what adversity reveals is lack within your soul—but lack
is not problematic to Jesus. Simply be honest with both yourself
and Him, and then set about correcting the deficit. I think also
that, amid the challenges, we discover a God who can be seriously trusted. When you are facing the heat of battle, remind
yourself of the three ancient Hebrew boys who were thrown
(quite literally) into a raging furnace by a crazed, self-obsessed
king because they refused to bow and deny their faith. The
story is recorded in Daniel 3. The miracle is that a "fourth person" was seen walking with them inside the furnace...and that
fourth person resembled the Son of Man (Jesus). He met them
in the fire.

Never forget, my friend, that Jesus will never abandon you.
Sometimes the path feels like sheer hell, but remind yourself
that He is familiar with every inch of that path. He waits ahead
for you, He walks beside you, and He is your rear guard when
needed. And if not him personally, then His ministering angels
(of which there are innumerable legions) are sent to escort and

protect you (Psalm 91). What a glorious thought. I hope you are feeling encouraged.

Brave isn't a fairy tale. I know there is a brave soul within you and you are braver than you realize. Brave resides within you because you are created in the image of the Most High God. Salvation is more than a mere statement of professed or preferred faith. Salvation is an ongoing and endless discovery of the benefits (and blessings) that come with a relationship with Jesus. If you are unsure of your own personal salvation, allow me to tell you that it takes only a "heartbeat prayer" to change that. Simply pause, look heavenward, and genuinely invite Jesus Christ into your heart to be Lord and Savior. Ask Him to forgive you of sin and independence (we are all sinners in need of a savior) and trust that if you ask, He will respond. Forgiveness is instant, you become a new creation, and a new path forward will open before you. It's incumbent on you then to take the next step and begin to walk in that path.

Brave within any true battlescape is a choice. Brave denies fear and rises—not in one's own strength but in the strength of Christ within. In my own strength I can do zero. In my own strength I fold and find myself saying, "I can't do this"—but when I draw upon His strength, when I remind myself that the Holy Spirit within is my Comforter and Helper, Strengthener and Advocate (see John 14:26), I find the resolve to press onward. I will write more of this in the chapter about staying within the divine exchange.

Smile and make mincemeat of your enemies. You are probably not going to find the word "mincemeat" in any translation of the

Bible. Mincemeat stems from my vivid imagination of that Psalm 23 table. When reteaching this point (at one of my earliest Colour Conferences) I may have found a meat cleaver (okay, I couldn't find a meat cleaver, but I found a bread knife—don't laugh) and I may have stood before the girls, waving my really scary bread knife and getting a little bit of attitude on toward the enemy. I may have thrust the point of the knife into the pulpit and said, "Devil…what you have meant for evil against us, God is going to turn to good. You are going to regret the day you messed with my father-in-law as a young man (because I believe it was the own inexcusable abuse he suffered that created brokenness, causing him to inexcusably act in ways that caused horror and brokenness in others). Enemy, we are going to take this insidious, horrible situation of sexual abuse that plagues society and we are going to turn it around and use this against you…We are going to out-wit and outlast you because of Jesus…And God is going to get the glory in people's lives…I'm going to take this (scary) bread knife and make mincemeat of your plans and strategies to harm humanity…and then make a meal of it for people…People are going to be restored, healed, and saved because of this!"

Yeah, I may have just done that nearly twenty years ago. The old bread knife (and come to think of it, I may have been wearing an apron someone gave me with Proverbs 31 verses on it) was just another way of wielding the "sword of the Spirit," which is part of the armor of God spoken of in Ephesians 6. The sword is the Word of God—His truth as opposed to the lie and His saving grace as opposed to the destructive strategies of darkness. Indeed.

And always remember to smile, my friend—the enemy hates it when we smile. I wrote of this in *The Sisterhood*, but nothing is more annoying than smiling soldiers. It's an act of faith, but it helps our battle stance. It's like the parent who comforts a distressed, disciplined, or injured child and then says, "Okay, smile now, come on, you can do it, smile." It's amazing how a smile can soften the harsh realities of the world and bring perspective. Psalm 34:5 in the Message says, "Look at him; give him your warmest smile. Never hide your feelings from him."

The lions are chained. Never forget "the lions are chained." It's a line from the famous allegory *Pilgrim's Progress*. On his celestial journey, Christian discovers there are indeed lions on the pathway, but he also discovers they are chained. Their roar was all they had. The Bible says that the devil prowls the earth seeking whom he may devour (1 Peter 5:8). His roar is louder than his bite, and his bite has been defeated at Calvary. Revelation aptly describes him as the "accuser of our brethren," who will one day be cast into deepest Hades (Revelation 12:10). All he has is accusation—and if there is no truth in the accusation, then there is nothing to fear.

Always remember, friend, that we have an enemy *who has been defeated but not destroyed.* As followers of Christ, we have the authority to defeat every strategy hatched in hell, and we do so according to authority in His Word, His blood, and His Glorious Name. That enemy, however, is not yet fully destroyed. One day he will be, but in the meantime, his noise, roar, and accusations have no legal authority in our lives as followers of Christ. However, that thought brings perspective to the world surrounding us, because there are many people who are not yet in Christ—they're unaware of the spiritual realm surrounding them. It's on their behalf that we need to step into the gap and pray. People are not likely to defeat an enemy that they barely believe exists, but we can do it on their behalf. That's where our prayers and intercessions for others matter so much. I'll enlarge these thoughts in coming chapters.

Grace, Grace to mountains of obstacles. In the Old Testament there is a profound verse relating to mountains and obstacles. In the context of rebuilding the temple, the Lord reminds his kingdom builders that when we are facing opposition, victory comes to us not according to might or power, but rather because of His Spirit present and at work in our circumstances. The verse goes on to prophesy that when the workers were to lay the top stone (or cornerstone), they should do so with shouts of "Grace, Grace":

> Then he said to me, "This is the word of the LORD to Zerubbabel: Not by might, nor by power, *but by my Spirit*, says the LORD of hosts. Who are you, O great mountain? Before Zerubbabel you shall become a plain. And he shall bring forward the top stone amid shouts of 'Grace, grace to it!'" (Zechariah 4:6–7 ESV; emphasis mine)

Zerubbabel is a picture of Jesus and His enabling work of grace within our lives. Before Zerubbabel (or Jesus), any mountains of obstacles become like leveled plains. Hebrews 12:24 reveals that in coming to Jesus we are now subject to a new covenant and a new charter to live by. It then says, "The murder of Jesus... became a *proclamation of grace*" (Heb. 12:24 MSG; emphasis mine).

A proclamation of grace! When I read these verses a few years ago, I started to quietly declare and proclaim "Grace, Grace" into the situations that were troubling or stretching me. I would literally visualize my beautiful Jesus going ahead of me and changing the dynamics in the room I was about to enter or the situations I was facing. Jesus gave us His Spirit, and said He would be like a traveling companion—He is with you and me right now in our present circumstances. He waits for us in our future and is already present on that path that winds before us. Learning to *proclaim His Lordship* is part of our battlescape arsenal—it acts as a powerful reminder within our own heart and spirit, and it acts to remind the opposition that we are not alone, that we are in and under the shadow of the Almighty, of whom it is said, "not by might, nor power, but by His spirit" (see Zech. 4:6).

STAY ON YOUR KNEES AND WAIT FOR THE PRINCE OF PEACE

As I bring this chapter to an end, I want to encourage you to live and walk in a stance of prayer, ever mindful and waiting for your Prince of Peace (Jesus) to lead and guide you.

My son Joel is a beautiful songwriter. I think many would concede that he is both poet and prophet on this front. He wrote a song called "Prince of Peace"—the lyrics are stunning, the convictions wherein it was written even more so. At the time, Brian and I were in the spiritual fight of our lives. Details are not necessary here, yet let me say that it felt like an assignment from hell was seeking to seriously hurt the bride of Christ in our nation, with consequent effects felt globally. Let's never be naive: If Satan seeks to kill and destroy Jesus, he will definitely go after and seek to hurt His bride, the church. In the same way he failed to destroy the Son of God, he will also fail to destroy the church whose heart is knit to her King.

Joel and the Hillsong UNITED team were in the final creative stages of the *Empires* album. Amid all the pressures and hidden labor in any project of this magnitude, Joel was praying, not only for his own father but also for some friends going through a difficult time. He was also very mindful of two Australians facing execution in Indonesia. A decade earlier, these two young men broke Indonesian drug laws and were facing the penalty of death. Their imprisonment stretched into a ten-year confinement, during which each came to Christ and sought to live rehabilitated within the prison system. On April 29, 2015, they lost their legal battle to have their death sentences reduced to a life sentence—and at 12:35 a.m. the two repentant, redeemed young men (with six others) walked into an execution yard. As they lifted trembling yet prepared hearts, they bravely and humbly sang "Amazing Grace"... and with the command of an executioner, they entered eternity. It was for his father, his friends, and these two boys that Joel wrote this song:

> *My heart a storm, clouds raging deep within*
> *The Prince of Peace came bursting through the wind*
> *The violent sky held its breath*
> *And in Your light I found rest*
> *Tearing through the night, riding on the storm*
> *Staring down the fight, my eyes found Yours*
> *Shining like the sun, striding through my fear*
> *The Prince of Peace met me there*
> *You heard my prayer*
> *Hope like the sun; light piercing through the dark*
> *The Prince of Peace came and broke into my heart*
> *The violent cross, the empty grave*

And in Your light I found grace
Your love surrounds me when my thoughts wage war
When night screams terror, there Your voice will roar
Come death or shadow, God I know Your light will meet
*   me there*
When fear comes knocking, there You'll be my guard
When day breeds trouble, there You'll hold my heart
Come storm or battle, God I know Your peace will meet
*   me there*
Again and again
Oh, be still my heart
And know that You are God
Oh fear no evil
For I know You are here
And my soul will know:
Your love surrounds me when my thoughts wage war
When night screams terror, there Your voice will roar
Come death or shadow, God I know Your light will meet
*   me there*
And my soul will know:
When fear comes knocking, there You'll be my guard
When day breeds trouble, there You'll hold my heart
Come storm or battle, God I know Your peace will meet
*   me there*
Oh, be still my heart
My soul will ever know that You are God
And You heard my prayer

—"PRINCE OF PEACE," WORDS AND MUSIC BY
JOEL HOUSTON, MATT CROCKER,
AND DYLAN THOMAS, 2015

Psalm 84 speaks of those who journey and pilgrim from strength to strength, increasing in victorious power. Life isn't always smooth or easy, and it doesn't always play out like we perhaps hope it will—but regardless, we have a Prince of Peace whose name is Jesus and whose promise is to never leave us or forsake us. When thoughts wage war, when fear comes knocking, or when the night season of adversity screams terror, I pray that a deep resolve will sustain and carry you safely.

I pray you are encouraged to remain within the battlescape. Allow the experience to refine and arm you for the path ahead, because quite possibly, your story of courage and victory will encourage countless others along the way.

FOUR

STAY WITHIN THE DREAMSCAPE

(Listen to the Wind Words)

Does life ever intrigue you?

As I open this chapter, I am sitting opposite my husband in a café in New York. We're here for one of the many conferences we host around the world. It's August and the summer vibe is tangible. The café is alive with chatter, the sidewalk outside busy with people intently headed "somewhere," and Brian is miles away, caught up in his own thoughts, daydreams, and phone (twenty-first-century life, right?). After forty years of marriage I'm at ease with the phone—it's office, newsfeed, precious sports editorial, plus pen and paper for the plethora of things that consume the visionary mindscape of my beloved. Observing my surroundings (and lost in my own thoughts), I may have randomly commented, "Life is a hive of activity." Miracle of miracles, he heard, looked up, and agreed.

I often find myself observing people, wondering who they might be, and even more, *what it is that consumes the busyness and industry of their lives.* As I look up from my own busyness of writing, the wind has picked up, leaves are flying in all directions, and the cover of cloud has changed the felt ambiance.

Life is indeed a hive of activity—and God's intent is that we each flourish and thrive in the midst of all we put our hand to. He created the planet to be fabulously occupied and enjoyed. In fact, in creation's "opening scenes," the mandate upon mankind was to multiply, fill the earth, and increase in every way (see Gen. 1.28). Many times throughout the history and journey of the Bible, we find God's heart toward the everydayness of our lives. In the Old Testament, no end of drama often accompanied the children of Israel's passage, and at one point His people are taken captive into Babylon. Yet the Father's desire still finds voice via the prophet of the day, Jeremiah, who said:

Build houses and make yourselves at home. Put in gardens and eat what grows in that country. Marry and have children. Encourage your children to marry and have children so that you'll thrive in that country and not waste away. Make yourselves at home there and work for the country's welfare. Pray for Babylon's well-being. If things go well for Babylon, things will go well for you. (Jeremiah 29:5–7 MSG)

In the New Testament book of Romans, Paul says it like this:

So here's what I want you to do, God helping you: Take
your everyday, ordinary life—your sleeping, eating, going-
to-work, and walking-around life—and place it before God
as an offering. Embracing what God does for you is the best
thing you can do for him. (Romans 12:1 MSG)

Take your everyday, ordinary life, place it before God as
an offering, and allow Him to help you. Take your everyday,
ordinary life, and be mindful that more surrounds you than
is obvious. Yes, build houses, have families, and "make yourselves at home"—but don't ever forget that a greater home
awaits you. Why does God constantly remind us of a *presence
and purpose* beyond this world? The answer: Because beyond
this normal, lovely, and everyday landscape is another landscape even more lovely and wondrous, a supernatural realm
wherein dreams, vision, and purpose enable us to live and walk
differently.

If my journey could teach you anything, I would say train
yourself to be conscious of this realm. Discipline yourself to
desire and look for the supernatural within the natural. Amid
the dreams and aspirations for yourself and your family, amid
study and inquiry, work and play, career and calling, amid fall-
ing in love and the inherent desire for babies and children, amid
gardens and houses and new-season wardrobes (hello), amid success and the attainment of all things related to being secure as
a human being—never forget that you have access to a realm
that is connected to the eternal and which is *your personal power
source* for all of the above. Therefore, friend:

AWAKE AND LISTEN TO THE
WIND WORDS

Awake to God's personal and perfect words for you—words
that enable you to successfully "stay the path" and accomplish
with ease what you have been placed on this planet to do.
God's desire is that you become a conqueror who will one day sit
down to a banquet dinner that, quite frankly, will blow all our
minds.

> *Are your ears awake?* Listen. Listen to the Wind Words,
> the Spirit blowing through the churches. I'm about to
> call each conqueror to dinner. I'm spreading a banquet of
> Tree-of-Life fruit, a supper plucked from God's orchard.
> (Revelation 2:7 MSG; emphasis mine)

So are your ears awake, my friend? Are you listening? Do you
have an ear to hear the Spirit blowing through the churches,
with insight and wonder just for you?

What does that actually mean? I believe these words are not
nestled in the last book of the Bible for idle rhyme or reason.
They're part of what is called "the Revelation of Jesus." They're
words that were entrusted to the banished and isolated Apostle John on the Isle of Patmos in the first century. The Bible
records that he was caught up in the Spirit on the Lord's day,
when suddenly he heard a voice behind him, a voice that told
him to write what he heard and saw, and then make it known to
the then (and future) church. The exhortation to "listen to the
Wind Words" (or to "the Spirit blowing through the churches")
repeats seven times. They're words that still apply, and they're

words that I believe can help keep us on track and give us direction in our pilgrimage through life.

I believe God's beautiful Holy Spirit is everywhere, seeking to speak and give direction—not in a weird or spooky way, but in a most natural and unforced way. I believe that every (local, healthy, and Christ-centered) church with a heart open to the Spirit is awash with these very "wind words" spoken of, words that bring wisdom and perspective, words that refresh the soul and invigorate our steps, words that identify with our everyday existence and bring direction from above. Words that are literally borne and carried by God's loving Holy Spirit right into our personal world. It's merely a case of whether we have the wherewithal to listen, perceive, and receive them.

Allow His outpoured Spirit to be helper and companion. I believe we are living in *the era of God's Spirit poured out*. If you are familiar with Scripture, you will know that Jesus (after accomplishing His seemingly insane mission of redemption) ascended back to the Father, but not before He gave very clear instruction to the disciples that they must wait for "another"—for the one who would help guide them thereafter (see John 14:16).

Jesus was leaving planet Earth, yet God chose not to leave humanity alone. Jesus was speaking of the Holy Spirit. Perhaps you are new to faith, so allow me to explain that the person of God is threefold—Father, Son, and Holy Spirit. They are equal to one another and yet each is magnificently unique. The Holy Spirit's felt outpouring (and presence) happened on what is now called the Day of Pentecost. The early disciples were gathered—120 in number, in an upper room in ancient Jerusalem—and *God's Holy Spirit came like fire.* It baptized (or immersed) them and they were never to be the same. They felt the sudden enabling that was promised to them (see John 14). They experienced the sudden *dunamis (dynamite) power* that explosively infused their inner soul and gained what was needed to continue their journey and mission. They were no longer alone, grieving the confusion, horror, and loss of their friend and Savior... *The Helper had come* and would remain with them as friend, companion, and source of all they needed.

I can't fully fathom what that day or moment was like. It certainly created no end of intrigue within the city and empowered those early Christians with a resolve that was breathtaking. It enabled them to live and walk and execute the exploits that became the foundations of the early church. Read of it yourself in the book of Acts (the acts of the early followers, the acts of the forerunners who *paved a way* for you and me, the acts that are still in play because we are still carrying Christ's name to a lost and dying world).

In all truthfulness, it was *the birth of a new era for the New Testament church*, an era of grace, covenant, power, and endless opportunity—an era that you and I are experiencing and still living in. That baptism of the promised Helper landed on each of the assembled disciples (Acts 2:3). It wasn't for a select few only. It was personal to each and every disciple gathered.

I want to encourage you that the one sent on that day of Pentecost is *your personal Helper and Companion* also. He has perfect "wind words" for you and your family, you and your circumstance, you and your journey. He resides in the presence of the Father and the Son, and He is the one who mediates between them and us, heaven and earth. He is the one who teaches, leads, and gives insight of the future (John 14:26). He is the one who listens to the conversations of heaven and then actions the heart of God thereafter. When you open your Bible for personal devotion, the Spirit is the one hovering nearby to quicken the Word. When you listen attentively to the words or wisdom of others, the Spirit is near, seeking to make their words resonate in your spirit. Again, He is the entrusted one who carries the wind words of heaven to you personally.

As I sit here (now on vacation in Italy, watching a balmy sky and listening for the perfect words to write onto this page for you), I want to encourage you to *reimagine your relationship with the Spirit of God.* I want to encourage you to approach the way you listen differently. When you open your Bible (which you may have been doing for a lifetime already), open it with a heightened mind-set that breath-of-God words are waiting for you. Open it with an expectation to hear God's voice like never before. When you turn up for church (and I hope you are constant in that habit), pay attention to all that is taking place. Listen with an attentiveness that believes wind words specific for you and your reality are in the air.

I've been a churchgoer for a bunch of years now. I have sat in a million meetings, listened to a million sermons, and opened my Bible (hopefully) a million times. Yet more than ever, *I hunger for truth.* I hunger and long for God's perfect and personal words—words that encourage my own daughter-heart, words that sustain and offer strength for the many things that consume my (busy and sometimes hectic) life, words that show me how to continue in my calling as wife, mother, and pastor. I encourage you to hunger also. Listen. Listen for God's heart of relationship toward you. Listen for His perfect perspective and direction. Listen for His promptings—because if ever there was a time to fine-tune our ears, it's now. "Speak, We're Listening" was the theme language over a recent Hillsong Conference (2015), but it's so much more than a passing theme. It is a conviction and stance of sweet surrender that will enable us all to "stay the path" and finish our race as intended.

Listen for the sake of others. The world is in need of many things—peace, hope, discernment, answers—but what this complex and wonderful world needs most is a global church full of genuine Christ followers who have an ear to His Spirit…an ear that can bring the goodness and kindness of God into the backyard of every neighborhood, village, city, and nation, ears that can hear the "prophetic heart of God" for people—again, not in a weird and strange way, but in a gracious way that arrests the human soul, enabling people to discover that there truly is a God in heaven who believes in them.

I'm grateful for the Spirit-inspired words I've heard over the years. They are words that at the time framed my own pathway, and then, because I have the privilege of teaching and pastoring, they're words that have in turn framed the lives of others.

When I was young and lacking in confidence about calling and ministry, I waited on a church altar, desperate for perspective. In the quietness, I heard, *"Bobbie, Brian's fruit is your fruit also."* They were "wind words" that brought release to my aching spirit. They framed my fledgling capacity to understand and release Brian into his calling, and in doing so, I found release. Today he and I (and an entire global church around the world) live in the fruit of that whisper.

When I was struggling in a young marriage and felt like I

had married the wrong guy (hello), it was the wind words of the Spirit that suggested I step onto higher ground and observe the prevailing conditions. Those words helped me see that I hadn't married the wrong person, but that the enemy was trying to create a wedge within our relationship. I took authority over any strategy of the enemy to create division, and literally overnight, the situation corrected.

It was the wind words blowing through a fairly normal Sunday service in the late nineties that gave me insight to the heart of God for His church. I sensed precise and clear words within my spirit: *"Bobbie, when I look at my beautiful people, I call them three things. I call them Family, Body, and House."* What followed (in that moment of quiet contemplation and conversation) became *a revelation of the Body of Christ* that enabled me to write a book called *Heaven Is in This House.* It's currently out of print, but definitely something I need to revisit someday. They were words that helped thousands around the world understand the church (including her health and her position in society) in a new light.

It was the words of this same Spirit many years ago that whispered, *"Be still and be silent—I will vindicate you."* It was our first encounter with disappointing conflict within our young ministry team. Distortion of truth and proverbial mud were flying everywhere. The human response is always to justify and defend, yet the wind words encouraged the opposite. As with everything, the wind words were right.

It was wind words that whispered only recently, *"Bobbie, I will never lose you to confusion."* I am somewhat of a perfectionist in that I labor intensely to bring my very best to the table. I was agonizing over the preparation needed for my twentieth year of

Colour Conference. There was so much to be accomplished in so little time. The wind words of His Spirit calmed *my* spirit in the midst of due diligence to give the girls the finest we could muster.

It was wind words around this same time that took notice of my ducks. Okay, feel free to laugh out loud! I confess, I am somewhat of a "ducks in a row" kind of girl. At the time, my "creative ducks" were in chaos—too many creative demands and projects swirling in my head. I honestly felt something within say, *"Okay, let's land these ducks, one duck at a time, and the Spirit will help."* Imagine that conversation in heaven. Hilarious. I know I have a vivid imagination, but I honestly believe God is totally on the page with our everyday (ridiculous) lives. Can you imagine that conversation in the throne room (or wherever they chat up there)? *"Her ducks are in chaos, we need to help the poor child!"*

Friend, I could go on and on. The actual "wind words" recorded in the book of Revelation are weighty and intense, but they were what the seven churches in that day needed to hear. God has perfect words for us today, and I encourage you to listen for them. If my journey could teach you anything, when it comes to the dreamscape of life, I would also say...

DON'T DISQUALIFY YOURSELF FROM DREAMING

The promise of the second chapter of Acts (trivia info: 2nd Chapter of Acts was also the name of a gospel group back in the seventies when I first got saved) is to everyone. The Word declares that in the last days, God will pour out His Spirit on *all* flesh—upon the sons and daughters, upon young and old alike, upon anyone who desires His truth (see Acts 2).

Before Jesus ushered in a new covenant and era, the Word of God was often described as "rare" or "hidden." It needed the prophets of old, or those specially anointed, to bring the Word into the lives of the everyday masses. Those times have changed. You have the capacity (in Christ) to hear God's heart for your life and calling. You have the capacity (in Christ) to dream dreams and see visions. Again, not in a way that makes one strange or odd, but in a way that "lights the path" not only for your own footsteps but for those you are called to influence along the way.

Ephesians 4 teaches that the "fivefold ministry gifts" (of apostle, prophet, pastor, teacher, and evangelist) are entrusted for the exhortation of the saints for "the work of the ministry." In other words, the *responsibility* of this path that we are all navigating interconnects and belongs to all of us. Yes, we are of course responsible for our own steps, but we are also responsible for the footsteps of those walking near or around us. The way I walk affects my husband, our children, and the church we pastor. We can influence people in a truly positive and fabulous way because of His Spirit in and upon us and because we have "eyes to see and comprehend," when others are perhaps blinded to the road they're on.

Do not disqualify yourself from being a person of influence in this regard. You have every right, as a follower of Jesus, to claim the wonder and power of Isaiah 61:

The Spirit of the Sovereign LORD is on me [*you*], because the LORD has anointed me [*you*] to proclaim good news to the poor. He has sent me [*you*] to bind up the brokenhearted, to proclaim freedom for the captives and release from darkness for the prisoners, to proclaim the year of the LORD's favor and the day of vengeance of our God, to comfort all who mourn, and provide for those who grieve in Zion—to bestow on them a crown of beauty instead of ashes, the oil of joy instead of mourning, and a garment of praise instead of a spirit of despair. [*Because of you*] They will be called oaks of righteousness, a planting of the LORD for the display of his splendor. (Isaiah 61:1–3 NIV; paraphrase and emphasis mine)

Imagine being the source of all that is mentioned in these verses above. Imagine encountering a brokenhearted person and having the ability to bind their hemorrhaging heart because you carry insight to God's goodness and "wind words" perfect for them. Imagine the Spirit alerting you to the captive on that road, and imagine Him giving you "wind word" perception on how to truly intervene and facilitate freedom. Imagine being the person who changes the atmosphere around you—the one who is marked with joy and gladness and who is a display of His splendor (read the verses above again). If my journey could teach you anything, I would encourage you to be the "atmosphere architects" on this glorious path home. I would also say…

Hang with the dreamers, and avoid the dream killers. Sadly, there are plenty of people who can't handle a dream of influence within the heart of another. The attitude, criticism, cold shoulder, or even contempt they might show is more about the deficit within their own heart than it is about you. Always remember that. It helps you to respond with grace rather than offense or hurt.

When I came to faith at age fifteen, I was in many ways a first-generation Christian in my family. It would be wrong of me to say that my parents did not have faith (who am I to judge?), but church life was not at the forefront of our little family. So when I encountered Christ as a schoolgirl in the early seventies and jumped, boots and all, into what was the "Jesus Revolution" sweeping across my nation, it created no end of intense family discussion among my aunties and cousins. My own mom and sister were okay with my conversion. However, some relatives were somewhat of another story. I remember my auntie Daphne (who was, by the way, lovely) cornering me on a Sunday afternoon. We had had a big family get-together one Sunday afternoon and I was keen to somehow find my way into the city for Sunday-night church. As I tried to figure how to catch a bus from Auntie Daph's house into downtown Auckland, I remember her quite scathingly saying, "Bobbie, if God is going to raise everybody from the dead...*where is he going to put them? They won't fit on the earth!*" Okay, I'm trying not to smile now as I write this, but, quite honestly, what an odd question to pose rather violently to a brand-new baby Christian. I can't remember if I answered her literally (probably not, because I would have chosen to be respectful), but inside my head I remember thinking, "I don't know, Auntie Daph...I guess if God can raise them from the dead, He can find a place for them."

Perhaps an odd story to recount from my past, but "dream killers" (of one sort or another) are always going to be around. In the early days, when Brian and I moved to Sydney to pioneer and begin our dream of planting a church, those same relatives remained dismissive of what was so close to my heart. I would travel back to New Zealand to visit (and show off my babies), and to be honest, some of that family refused to acknowledge our life in Australia. They never asked one question about Sydney, Brian, or what was becoming our life's work. I'm not wounded, but perhaps there are those close to you who don't understand the dreamscape of your life. Always be kind, always be gracious, always be understanding, because calling and destiny are a revelation. Perhaps the lights just haven't gone on for them (yet), but never allow the negative voices to deter you. Keep pressing on, and with time, they will understand as the fruit of your life proves that what you have devoted your life to is both important and weighty.

And if you are blessed (hallelujah!) to come from a nation that suffers from the "tall poppy syndrome," then be mindful that that mind-set can be painful at times. The tall poppy syndrome tends to diminish (or despise) anyone with an aspirational desire to succeed or be a blessing to others. It's a horrible reality. In our homeland of Australia it is far too prevalent, and we as a couple, family, and church have been attacked on this front many a time. In the cruelest sense, it is an anti-Christ spirit that hates the success and influence of the church. If you are in ministry and if what you do begins to take ground and bring Christ-centered change, then you will encounter it. Simply recognize it for what it is, and press on. To stay the path, you need to get good at recognizing (and ignoring) the unjustified critics and religious naysayers. Walk with purity and grace alongside the redeemed and unredeemed alike, exemplify Christ always, love your neighbors...and pray for your enemies.

And then finally, if my journey could teach you anything about the dreamscape of life, I would say...

*   *   *

Dream in full Technicolor. I speak of this a little within *The Sisterhood*. The word "manifest" is described (in Strong's Bible dictionary) as "the many tints and hues and colorful expressions of God entering the human arena." I have a confessed love affair with these words. If we were to peel back the layers of this (earthly) landscape in order to view the (spiritual) landscape that surrounds us, we would be overwhelmed with the wonder of color. The sounds and colors of heaven reveal the endless creative wonder of God Himself.

In the same way, when we engage God in His fullness (if that is remotely possible this side of eternity), we discover that life doesn't have to be dull and boring, lifeless and pointless. We discover life has many colors and much depth. We discover a God whose desire is that we experience the "exceeding, abundant and above" (see Eph. 3:20) of His reality within our lives. We discover a God full of visions and dreams, and things that enable us to color this world in remarkable ways.

Joseph in the Old Testament was a young man with the hand of God upon his life. He was marked for greatness—greatness that would bring solution to the (ancient) world he was born into. His young life engaged the "dreamscape" that had his name upon it. All hell came against him. His brothers (family, relatives—not sure if he had an Auntie Daph) were not happy. Long story short, they sold him into slavery, and yet amid the intense drama, he "stayed the path." He endured. He listened to the wind words that gave him perspective and direction, and he allowed the Spirit to be his personal Companion and Helper when brutally opposed and imprisoned. Big pic, young

Joseph went down in history as "the boy with the coat of many colors"—a coat (and calling) that his father bestowed upon him.

Allow the Spirit of God to bestow upon you His perfect will for your life. Allow Him to clothe you in the many wondrous layers and colors of His salvation. Stay the path, and should the ambiance of life change for the worse, as it did in that New York café when the wind picked up and the storm cloud rolled over... influence that changing landscape with the possibilities and testimony of your life.

FIVE

STAY IN LOVE

(Our Collective Breath)

Composer and author James McBride had it correct when he said, "Family love *is like the wind: instinctive, raw, fragile, beautiful, at times angry, but always unstoppable. It is our collective breath. It is the world's greatest force.*" I don't know what family represents for you personally, but in so many ways these words, that I often find myself returning to, describe perfectly the landscape of love within family.

The notion of love will incite a myriad of responses from people. Everyone's experience is different depending on upbringing or circumstance, yet *the need for and power of love is common to all.* Love is the foundational building block within the human soul. Its presence or absence is felt not only within every family unit on the earth but also within every culture and society that has ever existed. Lack or distortion thereof is the root cause of all heartache and pain. In a negative sense, the *love of money and power* (and inherent greed that often attaches itself) is at the core of most discord and war. The inflexible *love of self* is at the core of most relationship breakdown, and *love withheld* in any exchange of life will rob that exchange of its joy, hope, and potential.

I doubt that you would disagree that love is a powerful force—and *felt love* within the dynamic of family is crucial if we are to stay the path successfully. As McBride said, it is our collective breath and the world's greatest force—a force that can propel a person onward, sideline them, or worse still, completely knock them off course. I believe that as we follow Jesus, with His trustworthy Spirit pulsating within our lungs (and step), *we can become the world's greatest force*—an irresistible force for good that exemplifies the simplicity, purity, and power of love as the Father intended, and a force that can turn the most impossible of situations around.

As I speak of family and love, the subject might be pulling at some difficult heartstrings within you personally, but be encouraged, dear friend, because with God nothing is impossible (see Luke 1:37). As we allow ourselves to be constantly "found in Him" (again and again), it is remarkable what miracles are fashioned within that unfailing divine relationship that issues from a supernatural realm. Therefore, if my humble yet real journey could teach you a handful of things about the faithfulness of God's ways when it comes to family, I would say...

FAMILY IS NOT AN ACCIDENT OF NATURE

There isn't a single human being throughout the existence of humankind who had any say (whatsoever) over whose womb they were conceived in. Not one of us. We don't get to choose our parents. Nor do we get to choose our race, nationality, or even the nation in which we open our eyes and take our first breath. Realizing this would take the insidious and ugly power out of racism, classism, and prejudice that somehow thinks one is better or superior to another by reason of birth. Realizing this will also take some of the angst out of our own existence, especially if life has been tough for you.

I don't pretend to understand all the complexities of life. Life is neither fair nor an even playing field for the masses. As I write these words, the pastoral side of my heart is leaning toward those reading who have had a difficult life. If you've had it tough, or those around you were not who they should have been to you, I am so sorry. You deserve better. Everyone deserves a decent beginning. Everyone deserves to be valued and treated with love, grace, and goodness. No one deserves to be abused or used, and everyone deserves to have potential spoken into them. The good news, however, (and I don't write this lightly) is that there is always a way forward—from a bad life to a better life—if you have eyes to see and a heart to believe. With the help of the Holy Spirit, you have the capacity to move forward into God's perfect plan for your life. You have the capacity to turn the failings of life (or the intent of the enemy against you) into a testimony, and my prayer is that you will find the courage and strength to do so.

To stay the path successfully we need to realize that *the important relationships in life* are not a haphazard accident or chance of life. They are part of our personal landscape for a distinct reason. Paul, in Ephesians, speaks to us of being predestined according to his purposes. In the Message version, it says:

It's in Christ that we find out *who we are* and *what we are living for*. Long before we first heard of Christ and got our hopes up, *he had his eye on us*, had designs on us for glorious living, part of the overall purpose he is working out in *everything and everyone*. (Ephesians 1:11–12 MSG; emphasis mine)

There will always be some people we encounter or walk with for a season—but there are others who have been (divinely) assigned to walk near and alongside us for a lifetime. I speak of those with whom we share planting, purpose, destiny, and family—our children, our close friends, and the gorgeous people (and sphere of influence) within our local church and calling who are connected to the convictions of our heart.

Our lives are not just naturally knit—our lives are supernaturally knit because of the greater plan and purposes of God. For reasons that perhaps only eternity will reveal, God chooses to connect us with certain people, and we have a responsibility to steward those relationships. We have a responsibility to walk in a manner that enables them to walk confidently and correctly. Our steps affect their steps, our decisions affect their decisions, and our convictions either shape the convictions they live and prosper in, or not.

I fully realize that "my babies" were my babies, yet as they have grown into adulthood and flourished in their own personhood, I realize that they were never mine, or ours alone. They were always the sons and daughters of heaven above, carefully entrusted for a season. Brian and I got to share in their childhood and teenage years. We got to share in shaping their introduction to a relationship with God and their perceptions of life.

We got to help them navigate their early years—the highs and lows of growing up (with all the associated drama)—and then we got to fall in love with the people they've each chosen to do life alongside, not only their marriage partners but the rich canvas also of their friends and world of influence. And to be honest, as I see the unique calling upon each of them, as I see the gifts and measure they are now stewarding themselves and bringing to the table of their own generation, the thought that God would allow us to be a part of this is mind-blowing.

All relationships are important. I know we could minimize the collision of lives to mere coincidence. However, I believe greater design is always in play. Your relationships with the people around and about you are important. Again, they're not some haphazard accident. Maybe they're not particularly lovely or perfect right now, maybe you can't control the way people are responding to you or treating you, but you can control the way you treat and respond to them. In a noble sense, you can be the "unstoppable force of influence" upon them. You can be the architect of positive change and goodness. I encourage you to view the circumstances differently. I encourage you to be *the source of life in the relationships you hold*—sow kindness, goodness, and forgiveness, and somewhere down this crazy track called life, you will reap the benefits if you faint not.

Every step is important in this journey homeward. Every step affects others. If my journey could teach you anything, it would be to truly understand these dynamics. They temper life in a beautiful and honorable way and prove endlessly pleasing to the heart of God. In the context of marriage, family, and children, I would say...

FIRST LOVE IS MORE POWERFUL THAN WE REALIZE

A chapter titled "Stay in Love" suggests also that we can step out of love—and it is when we step away from these things that first captivated our passions that it can prove to be detrimental to the safety and longevity of those walking alongside.

The first "wind words" recorded in the book of Revelation are about first love. Jesus sends a letter to the church of Ephesus. With kindness, He loves and encourages them. He praises their courage and persistence, but then He draws attention to the very thing that will be their undoing if not attended to. In chapter 2, He says: "But I have this against you, that you have *abandoned* the love you had at first" (Rev. 2:4 esv; emphasis mine).

In the Message, it reads: "But you walked away from your first love—*why?* What's going on with you, anyway? Do you have any idea how far you've fallen? A Lucifer fall! *Turn back!* Recover your dear early love. No time to waste" (Rev. 2:4–5 msg; emphasis mine).

Strong words. Turn back and recover your early love.

To lose or displace something is one thing, but to "walk away" or "abandon" something is quite different. The world is a series of relational tragedies in motion because too many people allow the normal and natural tensions of life to dictate their responses, and then in the momentary fireworks or fallout that can result, they abandon or walk away from what is relationally so important. At the first sign of independence within normally compliant children, parents overreact, and instead of "healthy teenage questions" being an opportunity for gracious conversation, arguments ensue and unnecessary drama enters the equation. Parents and children suddenly find themselves out of step with one another, and if it is not attended to quickly (and wisely), that glorious first love that has held them as dear family becomes compromised and threatened. Instead of healthy inquiry being a pathway to wisdom and maturity in young people, it becomes *a pathway of offense and rebellion*—and for the record, offense and rebellion carry a hefty price tag.

When that prophet lady spoke over my life (see chapter 1), she prophesied, "Your children will know no rebellion." Perhaps an unusual thing to say, but I have always understood its greater and deeper meaning. It has shaped my desire as a parent (and as a church leader) to create the kind of environment that allows our kids (natural and spiritual) to grow up and find their feet—an environment that allows them to ask questions about faith and find their own true north when it comes to that very same faith.

When our daughter, Laura, was a teenager, she once said to me, "Mum, it's not that I really want to go to a nightclub, but I just want to see what happens inside." She wasn't rebelling—she was just being a normal inquisitive teenager. Sometimes as parents, we need to lighten up, trust God, and allow our kids to figure on their own a few things about life. If we have done our honest best as parents, if we have sought to tenderly train them as the Bible instructs—"Train up a child in the way he should go: and when he is old, he will not depart from it" (Prov. 22:6 KJV)—then when they do test the waters of so-called life or worldliness, they won't be fooled or seduced by it. They'll make their own wise judgments.

The Bible says, "O taste and see that the LORD is good" (Ps. 34:8 KJV). I love that verse. I love that people (outside of faith) walk into our churches and lives and literally taste the goodness of God. As with my own experience of coming to faith, they can't totally explain it at first; all they know is that it tastes good and right. Well, sometimes our babies (who have been raised within the safety of fabulous church life) also need to "taste and see that the world is *not* so good." As parents, we can tell them that so many things (outside of faith) are empty, shallow, and ultimately dangerous, but there comes a moment when they need to figure and discover it for themselves.

One of our great young campus pastors came into the back room of church one night. She and her husband have four little girls. One of them had made a decision for Jesus that night in kids church. So cute, with a "kid's decision card" to bear witness to the very special moment. Danielle wasn't dismissive of what her little girl had done, but she may have quietly joked with me (wink, wink) that she wasn't exactly sure that her little "wild child" had gotten saved either. I remember encouraging her that more than likely she had. So often, our babies do make genuine and real decisions to invite Jesus into their heart when they are little. If they invite Him to be their Savior, then He surely will. Jesus loves children and is recorded as saying in the gospels, "Suffer [or allow] the children to come unto me" (Mark 10:14 YLT), but somewhere farther down the track of life, often when they are teenagers and when all their friends are deciding which way to go in life, those children will decide (or not) to become "followers." And, parents, that's the truly important decision. That's the decision that we must always be praying for.

All our three children (who are serving God in powerful ways today) had a moment of truth in their teenage years—a moment that defined their personal resolve to love, seek, and

serve God. At the time, Brian and I were so grateful for the rein-
forcement of a healthy youth group within that equation. So,
parents: When the heat is on, when tensions rise and potential
discord is in the air, when the temptation presents to lord it over
your kids because you're the parent and they're not—always be
mindful of protecting that precious "first love." That first love
that (within marriage) walked you down the aisle and had you
romantically reciting "for better, for worse, for richer, for poorer,
in sickness and in health," or that first love that took your breath
away as you held for the first time that fragile and newborn baby
son or daughter.

As parents, it is our responsibility to steward first love to
maturity. As parents, it is our responsibility to choose wisely
when our kids can't or won't or don't know how. As parents, we
play such a critical role in helping our families "stay the path."
And when we choose to think generationally, it never ever quite
ends. I'm now watching my children navigate their own children. By way of testimony, we are all tracking the same pathway
home (smile and say hallelujah, Bobbie), but as a "Grammie" to
seven little poppets, I watch intently. When I'm asked for wisdom by their parents, I want to have it readily within my experience to offer, and I want to do so with grace. And when they
don't ask, I choose to be okay with that also. I don't want to be
the high-maintenance, interfering in-law or grandmother. I trust
the deposit of God within my children to get it right, and I pray
intently that heaven's wind words will guide them perfectly, in
the same way they have helped guide Brian and me.

And never forget that God is well able to watch over your
babies. He actually loves them more than you do and is fiercely
committed to their well-being and safety. If He has a lifeline

of communication (relationship) with you as a parent, He can alert you to danger. I recall two specific occasions where the Holy Spirit literally did that with our children. One was as we were traveling across America. Somewhere in transit, the Spirit arrested Brian's attention—Laura was in trouble at home. A series of urgent phone calls from Dallas airport to my personal assistant in Sydney enabled us to intervene. As we arrived, jet-lagged and exhausted, in Canada, my husband phoned our daughter from our hotel room. I will never forget the moment. It was three a.m. As I sat on the edge of the bed and listened to Brian talk to his baby girl, I would have gotten back on that plane and flown twenty hours back home. Laura had fallen into an almost compromising situation, and she was so very, very grateful that her daddy had an ear to her Heavenly Daddy, who cared about her in that moment. Together, her daddy and her "Abba" (Heavenly Daddy) were able to save her from a difficult situation.

The second was a similar situation. We were ministering in Seattle, and a gentleman approached us in an early morning prayer meeting. He asked to pray for our children. At first I was a little defensive (sorry). I may have said, "My kids are fine." Nevertheless, he persisted and we prayed. Unbeknown to us, our son Ben was in a horrific situation playing out at home. It involved the tragic accident of one of his schoolmates and Ben's pastoral heart (even back then) to intervene and help. Our son was at a crossroads in his own experience, and the Holy Spirit knew. He intervened, and I have no doubt that the prayer of an obedient gentleman in Seattle helped. So do your best as parents, but know also that as we commit them to God, He is well able to watch over them. He has a bird's-eye view. So even when you don't know where they are, He does. Hence our responsibility to be praying parents.

First love is felt across so many layers of life. Never forget why you fell in love. Life in a fallen world can so easily taint the things that are important. Left to itself, the paint on a house will corrode and splinter, and left to itself, any relationship can and will feel the effects of time and distance. That's why it's important to walk with the Spirit of God and constantly live in the Word, because the Spirit acts as umpire in our lives, ever reminding us of what's important and needful. That's why it's important to make regular deposits into every relationship, because if you don't, you may wake up one day to a seriously "bankrupt" and desolate relationship. With regards to family and love, I would also say . . .

THE HIGHER WAY NEVER FAILS

Proverbs 14:12 says, "There is a *way* which seems right to a man, but in the end it leads to death" (NHEB; emphasis mine).

Isaiah 55:9 says, "As the heavens are higher than the earth, so are *my ways* higher than your ways and my thoughts than your thoughts" (NIV; emphasis mine).

Isn't it grand and reassuring to know there is a "higher way"? Especially when you have exhausted (without much success) your own avenues of doing. I don't want to have a relationship with God that is restricted to merely acknowledging Him as Savior of my life—I want to have an ongoing, vital, and exciting *relationship with His ways*. I want to learn of Him and have the insight to choose His higher way at every bend and curve of life, because after walking with Jesus for forty-five years, after watching him work in my own life and in the lives of others, I am of the conviction that His way will always keep the path safe and sound and moving forward. Therefore, beloved friend...

Love tenderly. When harshness wants the upper hand, resist and choose the way of Christ. He only ever responded tenderly and beautifully toward people. He wasn't afraid to call the pot black, he wasn't afraid to call sin out, he wasn't afraid to rebuke and correct bad behavior (especially ugly religious behavior)—but throughout the Bible account, Jesus always responded tenderly to people.

When it comes to those alongside us in life, choose tenderness before anything else. Tenderness inquires calmly and intelligently before exploding in presumption. Tenderness looks for what might be happening beneath the surface before it judges what is happening *on* the surface, and tenderness always brings grace into the equation.

Forgive easily. It's easy to hold a grudge, but where's the love or life in that? Discipline yourself to forgive easily and quickly. You'll release others and yourself. When we fail to forgive, we hold ourselves—and those we are unforgiving toward—in a prison (see Matt. 18:21–35). Forgiveness allows the path to go forward for people. Forgiveness is not always a natural response, which is why we need Christ within to help us. If you are a victim to unforgiveness, then I pray that God will make a way for you and that He will give you wisdom and courage to press on regardless. And if you are holding unforgiveness toward another, then I encourage you, dear one, let it go. Let it go, let it go, let it go.

*   *   *

Encourage always. Would you agree that people who encourage are like a breath of fresh air? However, let's be honest: Encouragement is not always the natural first response of everyone. There are some people who just seem to slide out of bed with sunshine in their eyes, and then there are others who just slide out of bed. Not everyone sees the light in the day, the moment, or the conversation.

I believe encouragement is a learned discipline also. We can choose to bring a little ray of sunshine into the room, or we can be "killjoy grumpy pants" who walk the gray clouds in. How lovely to be the one upon the path who is endlessly encouraging, the one who will always say, "You can do this... You got this, baby." I've got people in my world exactly like this. But they weren't necessarily born with a happy gene. For the most part, they've chosen encouragement and joy as a discipline within their "daily discipline."

Growing up, I tended to be slightly pessimistic about life, mainly because I had a fear of being disappointed. I didn't want to hope too much, for fear that something hoped for would not happen. But in Christ, those (death) dynamics were replaced with life dynamics. Can I remind you that Jesus came to give "life and life in abundance" (see John 10:10)? So among your friends, become the fun master, the social secretary, the instigator of joy and encouragement, and the one who always sees endless possibility. It's not superficial hype—it's faith in motion.

And in case you haven't been told lately that you are amazing and wonderful—I'm telling you now! You are amazing, capable, intelligent, and well able. You have within you the capacity to be a "well" of life and an oasis of joy on this glorious path home.

*   *   *

Choose to believe the best of people. One of the disappointing taints upon the church today (often seen in social media because anyone, it seems, can open a media app and pontificate away) is so-called Christians who leap to believe the worst of people before they remotely know the facts. It's a nasty spirit and it reflects nothing of the nature or kindness of Christ. If anything will divert people from the pathway (or worse still, prevent others from even desiring this Christian life), it's gossip, innuendo, and harsh talk that is so destructive. The higher way is to choose to believe the best of people. The higher way is to know the facts before you pass judgment, and even then, better not to pass judgment at all. Better to quietly pray and be an advocate of what is positive and good. If you can't say anything nice about someone, don't say anything. Our role (as followers of Christ) is to unconditionally love people to healing, wholeness, and safe arrival. It is to remember always that God is still at work within all of us, and if it weren't for the grace of God, where would any of us be?

Be content that while it is still day, it is still a day of grace for all (see John 9:4). Be the one who doesn't enter into the critical conversation. It's amazing how silence on someone's part makes the negative conversation awkward and thwarts a destructive thread of gossip going further. And let's always remember that sometime down the track there will be a day of accountability for all of us, so let's practice grace and do unto others as we would have them do unto us (see Matt. 7:12).

And finally, don't allow mistakes, imperfections, and margins to hijack the potential and wonder of life. Let me explain. We all make mistakes. You can't be human without making mistakes. Mistakes don't frighten or shock God, and mistakes within the human experience should not penalize those involved. Mistakes are how we learn in life. The challenge is to learn from life and not continue making the *same* mistakes.

Imperfections are also the landscape of normal and natural life. We all have different strengths and attributes. Don't write people off because their strengths within a certain realm or situation aren't what you expected. Life is about ebb and flow and learning to work together. Within our Hillsong ministry we honestly do not look for perfection in people. We pay more attention to a person's heart and soul, including whether or not they have a teachable spirit and a desire to grow. We encourage people to simply bring their best to God (not to us)—and whatever that looks like becomes an offering of the heart and a sweet-smelling fragrance to the Father. God has a remarkable way of taking our humble best and compensating for any deficit with His miracle-working grace. Brian will often say of our family and church that we are all overachievers because of His grace.

Imperfections within everyday family life are what make family so colorful, crazy, and beautiful. They make us who we are as the human race, and in the broadest sense they are what allows grace (and all her glorious attributes) something to work upon. Our imperfections attract the perfection of His goodness, and our weaknesses are what make His strength so remarkable.

Margins, however, are different. Life allows margin for error, but maturity demands we grow in wisdom and reduce those margins of error. As we take responsibility for those alongside and for the important things entrusted to us, our margins for error do

STAY THE PATH   81

change and require of us a different standard—a standard that, I might add, we are capable of reaching.

As a wife and mother, and as a pastor and leader, I choose to hunger and thirst after wisdom and integrity so that I don't stuff up and compromise the precious treasure entrusted. Always remember that opportunity and blessing come with account-ability. If you are a new mom or dad, then you can afford to make some mistakes because children can be wonderfully for-giving (and let's face it, those newborns don't exactly come with an instruction manual). But if you are in your fifties or sixties (for example), let's hope you've got some wisdom up your sleeve. In the same way, if you are young into ministry you may have some room for error (although today the less-than-gracious, mean-spirited watchdogs of Christianity are fairly brutal), but again, as platform and influence increase, the stakes of ministry also change. Margin for error alters, and we all need to remem-ber that.

Turn the page and allow me to continue, because life is an endless landscape of bends and curves, leading ever upward and onward. God knows the pathway inside and out, and He has purposed so many dynamics that will give you good success along the way. One of those dynamics is to understand the soil you find yourself within.

SIX

STAY WITHIN THE SOIL

(Gardens, Fields, and Vineyards)

H e motioned me to look up and over my shoulder. He knew I would like what I saw behind me.

The boss and I had decided to trade the familiarity of dinner in our hotel for something more quintessential and local down the street. The short walk down the hill and into the little cobblestone laneways was lovely. The temp was perfect (no humidity hair) and my post-conference aching feet were happy to be in a pair of faithful and comfy Birkies.

The challenge of any Italian seaside town is the mystery of where to eat. We've learned to avoid the tourist spots and aim for wherever the real locals are eating. The little wine shop in the tiny lane had tables and looked inviting. The menu was small, but I may have (seriously) eaten the best pesto pasta in the history of the universe. As we sat in the relaxed atmosphere, happy to be on vacation in such a gorgeous part of the world, Brian motioned to what was behind me. Hanging just inside the entry, and not visible to those passing by outside, was the most beautiful painting. In earth and muted tones it captured the aged and rugged hand of a vinedresser or farmer. With dirt under his nails and within the deepened crevices of his skin, he held a cluster of rich, ripe, purple grapes. Brian knew I would love it for all the reasons I am about to give expression to.

Every human heart and every relationship is a garden, a field, and a vineyard. Every nation and landmass on this big blue planet has wonder and potential within her soil. Mankind was created for Eden, and Eden for mankind. The psalmist declares that "The earth is the LORD's and the fullness thereof" (Ps. 24:1 ESV). Earth was created for splendor, and the splendor of the earth is found in the fullness of Christ. When the fullness of Christ takes residence within the human heart, when it begins to water and tend the gardens and fields of our lives, and when it truly radiates from within His bride, enabling her to become the catalyst of change she is designed to be...*then the earth will become the vineyard He had in mind.* The earth and her immense fullness will return to the essence of Eden's intent.

Life was never intended to be hard. It was never intended to be a desolate or barren wasteland in need of hard labor, tears, and prayer. In fact, the heart of God is found once again in the fifth chapter of Isaiah. It speaks of a divine desire for a certain vineyard. It speaks of a vinedresser who gave all in order that his vineyard would bring forth its finest, yet amid all that was done for it, the vineyard somehow failed to produce its potential. Instead of a vintage crop, it brought forth a harvest that was sour to the taste and disappointing to the one who planted it.

The metaphor is strong.

Isaiah, under the inspiration of the wind words of his day, writes:

> I'll sing a ballad to the one I love, a love ballad about his vineyard: The one I love had a vineyard, a fine, well-placed vineyard. He hoed the soil and pulled the weeds, and planted the very best vines. He built a lookout, built a winepress, a vineyard to be proud of. He looked for a vintage yield of grapes, but for all his pains he got junk grapes. "Now listen to what I'm telling you, you who live in Jerusalem and Judah. What do you think is going on between me and my vineyard? Can you think of anything I could have done to my vineyard that I didn't do? When I expected good grapes, why did I get bitter grapes?" (Isaiah 5:1–4 MSG)

Isaiah's words are beautiful, yet challenging. They speak of God's great love toward us. However, they also speak of our responsibility toward Him and all He has done for us. In the passage, it says that the owner planted the choicest vines in a vineyard that he had meticulously chosen—a fine, well-placed vineyard, to be precise. It tells how he labored to pull the weeds and remove the stones, and how he built a watchtower and winepress. The watchtowers of old were centric for protection, a place where the owner or guardian could watch against foxes that could spoil the vine or enemies with ignoble intent. The winepress of ancient times was designed so that the grape could be pressed of its precious juice within the actual field it was planted in.

We are living in an age where this analogy or metaphor still applies, an age that is more resourced with biblical wisdom and care than any other before us. We have easy access to the "choicest vines" of teaching and input that can protect our lives and cause us to be fruitful. In so many ways, *we have no excuse*. If you possess the power of choice (and most of us do), you have the ability to seek, search, and find wisdom about pretty much anything relating to life. So if my journey could teach you anything in this context, I would remind you that...

YOU ARE A VINEYARD WAITING TO HAPPEN

You are a vineyard with endless vines within your sphere. If you are facing challenges within the "vineyard of marriage," an ocean of good people exist who can speak into your life and give you solid biblical keys to go forward. If you are banging your head against the wall with issues relating to teenagers or small children, there are accessible pathways to better parenting. If you've dug yourself into a financial hole, or little foxes have come in and created havoc, there is godly wisdom available on how to climb your way back—and if you are in the vineyard of ministry, feeling isolated or stuck in your responsibility toward a congregation or community of people, then take heart from one minister to another. I'm here to tell you that there is always a way forward, and God has good people along this pathway who can help. Again, if you are living in the free world, you have the ability to "plant or replant" yourself into the wisdom and ways of God that yield the right fruit in our lives.

I say this because that is what God is asking (and declaring) in Isaiah: "*Can you think of anything I could have done to my vineyard that I didn't do?"* Our gracious God has done all He can do. He gave His Son and purchased our redemption (allow that to resonate; it will shoot faith-adrenaline into your soul). He gave us His Spirit, poured out to lead and teach us with those glorious "wind words" already spoken of. He gave us His time-less and infallible Word, full and overflowing with knowledge, understanding, and wisdom. The Psalms and Proverbs alone are a lifetime seminar, if you have a heart to seek them out. And He gave us His church. Now, I agree that not every church is perfect, yet when any local church seeks to be healthy and Christ-centered (and is doing her honest best), then God will cause that local church environment to become the family and community perfect for your journey.

You are *a stunning vineyard waiting to happen.* Don't negate these words because you feel unworthy. Don't reduce this truth because of what your life may look like now. Condemnation and hopelessness are the work of the enemy. So resist, and believe me when I say you are capable of a vintage crop—a vintage crop of a fulfilling, fun, meaningful (and sexy) marriage; a vintage crop of kids who grow up and become fabulous human beings and citizens of planet Earth; a vintage crop of perfectly matured and executed dreams and aspirations. Delight yourself in the Lord, and He will give you the desires of your heart (see Ps. 37:4).

Have you ever seen a vineyard in the height of splendor? Lush, green, mature, with succulent ripe grapes that when pressed bring forth the finest juice? I dare you to believe that you can be such a vine. For years I've wanted to do a photo shoot for my Colour girls in the vineyards of the world, simply because of the canvas it would paint. I find the imagery of a rich rolling landscape, flourishing under His care, irresistible. Regardless of what season the vine is in (summer, winter, spring, fall), there is confidence that every season has its design and purpose. And even if the vine has been spoiled in some way, don't ever forget that God is the one who can restore what the invasive worm has stolen (see Joel 2:25). He's the God who can turn any situation around. The Old Testament is basically a long historical account of the Father's endless devotion and ability to turn the bleak, barren, assailed (and often even rebellious) vineyard of His people back to their potential.

SEED IS NOTHING WITHOUT SOIL

Always remember that seed is nothing without soil.

Perhaps an obvious statement, but you would be amazed at how many good people try to flourish outside of being planted. I'm not saying this because I'm a local church pastor with a bias toward loyal church attendance—I'm saying it because it's a clear instruction within the Word of God that honestly keeps people safe upon the path.

Psalm 92 and Hebrews 10 are foundational verses on this note. Don't be tempted to switch off here (smile), because I promise you, friend, one of the main reasons our church can testify longevity and blessing on so many fronts is because of a deep revelation of these two chapters alone. Hillsong is not perfect, but she is a beautiful and fruitful vine because at the core of who we are as a body of believers is the revelation that planting is not only important to God but also critical to us as His children.

The book of Hebrews says, "Let us hold fast the confession of our hope without wavering" (Heb. 10:23 ESV). An amazing verse: to hold fast to hope without wavering—wow! We live in a world that is reeling under the weight of hopelessness, a world that is constantly wavering because people don't know who or what to trust. To possess an unwavering hope will hold you secure upon the path that this entire book is devoted to. The verse continues: "for he who promised is faithful. And let us consider how to stir up one another to love and good works, not neglecting to meet together, as is the habit of some, but encouraging one another, and all the more as you see the Day drawing near" (Heb. 10:23–25 ESV).

Never lose sight of the one who is faithful, and take careful notice of the clear and unmistakable instruction about not neglecting to gather to the House of God.

A glorious day is approaching, and I believe that those who recognize this truth and then abide in the planting of His choice for them will be the ones who will remain stable and secure when that day arrives. Of course, that day is somewhat of a mystery. However, the Bible is clear that the times surrounding it will be turbulent. It's those who are displaced (and not in regular and healthy attendance) who might find those days difficult. Why? Because God knows what it takes to safeguard the human soul. And, of course, Psalm 92 is epic in this regard. Interestingly, it's named "A Song for the Sabbath." Therefore, if my love affair with the House of God could teach you anything, I would say discover this psalm and allow wisdom for the journey to be engraved upon your heart.

It is good to praise the LORD and make music to your name, O Most High, proclaiming your love in the morning and your faithfulness at night, to the music of the ten-stringed lyre and the melody of the harp. For you make me glad by your deeds, LORD; I sing for joy at what your hands have done. How great are your works, LORD, how profound your thoughts! Senseless people do not know, fools do not understand, that though the wicked spring up like grass and all evildoers flourish, they will be destroyed forever. But you, LORD, are forever exalted. For surely your enemies, LORD, surely your enemies will perish; all evildoers will be scattered. You have exalted my horn like that of a wild ox; fine oils have been poured on me. My eyes have seen the defeat of my adversaries; my ears have heard the rout of my wicked foes.

The righteous will flourish like a palm tree, they will grow like a cedar of Lebanon; *planted in the house of the* LORD, they will flourish in the courts of our God. They will still bear fruit in old age, they will stay fresh and green, proclaiming, "The LORD is upright; he is my Rock, and there is no wickedness in him." (Psalm 92:1–15 NIV; emphasis mine)

This psalm never grows old. My prayer for you is that you'll find your planting, and that as you do, you will flourish and bear fruit well into old age. My prayer is that your heart and spirit (including a passionate desire for life) will remain fresh and green and that you'll be of irresistible vintage crop inspiration to others.

So just for the record:

Planting is your responsibility. You have the ability to decide where and how you sow your life, and God's Spirit is well able to lead you in such an important decision. Therefore, commit your way unto Him and He will direct your steps (see Ps. 37:5). Lean toward people who inspire you for all the right reasons. Find your tribe—great people who love God and have a sense of purpose surging through their veins—and then love that tribe. Planting is about godly fellowship and purpose, and all the fabulous ebb and flow within that.

Planting affects those around you. Where you allow your life to fall or land is important. If you are blessed to have a family, then where you are planted (especially when it comes to the House of God) is critical. Over many years of ministry, we have seen families lose their children to the things of God because parents foolishly uprooted their kids from the right planting. Life is full of seasons, and sometimes those seasons move us geographically, but always consider the spiritual environment of what you might be leaving or going to.

Stay within the soil of God's Word. Nothing shapes, transforms, and corrects our lives like the Bible. Psalm 119:105 says: "Thy Word is a lamp unto my feet, and a light unto my path."

The Bible is referred to as our "daily bread" for a reason. Neglect it and you will become malnourished, and malnourished is no recipe for living an abundant life. If you don't know how to read your Bible, or if it feels dry, switch between some of the different and wonderful translations available. The truth remains constant in all. Some translations are stronger study Bibles, while some paraphrases (such as the Message) bring the Word into everyday street language and are often refreshing. Have a few and use them together to gain a greater understanding of what the Word is actually saying to you.

Stay within the soil of right relationships. I spoke of relationships in the previous chapter—the people who are your destiny
friends and destiny partners along that road. My husband always
says, "Choose friends who will be a friend to your God-given
destiny." And of course, the question is: How do you do that?
Observe their passions, their habits, what's important to them,
and the fruit of their lives. Are they in step with the heart of God
and in step with the convictions that are truly important to you?

And on that note, allow new relationships time to develop.

When our son Joel met and fell in love with his wife, we
hardly knew this striking girl who had suddenly swept my son
off his feet (plus the reality that our family lives in different
corners of the planet didn't help the process of getting to know
her). Brian and I adore Esther, but for a split second (as a mom)
I didn't know if this beautiful young woman would be a friend
to the calling upon his life. Of course, she is more than perfect
alongside him, with much treasure within her own story that
Joel is equally committed to. I share this example only because
some parents are too fast and vocal about writing off the choices
their babies make of who they might desire to spend their lives
with. I know there is a natural instinct within parents to protect,
but nevertheless, trust and give any new relationship a chance.
I was a Jesus-Revolution, newly saved, first-generation Christian
myself, and I know for a fact that Brian's father didn't overly
warm to me the first time we met (I know... "How is that possible?" I hear you say). I was seventeen and apparently wore too
much green eye shadow for his liking—however, in all fairness,
he was probably only being protective in the same way we all are
of our children.

TRUST THE GARDENER

Trust the Gardener, dear friend. Trust Him in the same way that you can trust Him as the Potter who only has something beautiful in mind for the clay. Like the painting in the little Italian wine shop—trust His strong and yet gentle hands to bring you to maturity.

Trust His tenderness. The song of the Beloved (in Isaiah 5) is described as a *tender song* in the Amplified (Classic edition) translation. Everything about the Lord is tender, yet in His tenderness, He is not afraid to prune our lives of things that are, or will be, detrimental. He is also not afraid to prune our branches, because He knows there is more within when it comes to new growth and vision. If you do have a green thumb and love natural gardening, you will totally agree. Careful and correct pruning at the end of one season and before the next season is crucial to a healthy and beautiful plant. And you know I am not speaking of rose bushes and peach trees.

His intent is that you are *beautiful*. Beautiful in Greek is *hóraios*. It means "belonging to the right hour or season (timely)…flourishing…beautiful" (*Strong's Concordance* 5611). The promise of Psalm 144 captures this picture and declares that when our sons and daughters mature as intended, then the blessing is felt in the streets:

Then our sons in their youth will be like well-nurtured plants, and our daughters will be like pillars carved to adorn a palace. Our barns will be filled with every kind of provision. Our sheep will increase by thousands, by tens of thousands in our fields; our oxen will draw heavy loads. There will be no breaching of walls, no going into captivity, no cry of distress in our streets. Blessed is the people of whom this is true; blessed is the people whose God is the LORD. (Psalm 144:12–15 NIV)

Trust His correction. Jesus held nothing back on this subject. In the Gospel of John, His words are laid out plain and clear. Pruned if you do, pruned if you don't. He reminds us that He is the vine and the Father is the farmer who is not afraid to do what is best for the vine:

I am the Real Vine and my Father is the Farmer. He cuts off every branch of me that *doesn't* bear grapes. And every branch that is grape-bearing he prunes back *so it will bear even more.* You are already pruned back by the message I have spoken. Live in me. Make your home in me just as I do in you. In the same way that a branch can't bear grapes by itself but only by being joined to the vine, you can't bear fruit unless you are joined with me. I am the Vine, *you* are the branches. When you're joined with me and I with you, the relation intimate and organic, the *harvest is sure to be abundant.* Separated, you can't produce a thing. Anyone who separates from me is deadwood, gathered up and thrown on the bonfire. But if you make yourselves at home with me and my words are at home in you, you can be sure that whatever you ask will be listened to and acted upon. This is how my Father shows who he is—when you produce grapes, when you mature as my disciples. (John 15:1–8 MSG; emphasis mine)

Trust the soil. Trust the soil that you find yourself within. If you have a conviction about where you are sowing your life, then trust the conviction that positions you. Don't fear the soil or what it may require of you, and always remember: The devil cannot uproot what has been planted by God.

Our planting for the greater part of our adult life has been the nation of Australia. I was twenty-one when we moved there. Our world is broader and more global these days, but Brian and I will always call Australia home. I love the big island continent that she is. I love the people. I love that Aussies are free-spirited and that we speak our own version of English. I recall Esther (our Brazilian daughter-in-law, who I just spoke of) telling me that talking to Joel on the phone in the early days of their romance was impossible. On one occasion, she said, "Joel, I have no idea what you are saying…Hang up and text me."

I love Aussie mateship and the loyalty that pervades our nation. I love that when she was discovered by Europeans in 1606, she was named Australia del Espiritu Santo or literally "the southern land of the Holy Spirit." However, without doubt there is also a strong humanistic, anti-Christ force at work in our land. Aspects of that contentious spirit have caused angst and heartache, some of which I shared in chapter 3. I say all this because I could easily draw back from aspects of that planting. I could easily fear the cost (and the personal price tag) involved in persevering to build His kingdom and testimony in our land. Yet Isaiah 61 reminds me that God has a plan for the entire earth. His desire is that righteousness will come to full bloom and that

His praise will go on display before the nations (see Isa. 61). His desire is that the cities and villages of our planting will become an irresistible garden of His goodness and possibilities. I remind myself of the 1606 declaration (Australia, the southern land of the Holy Spirit) and I stir up my praying heart for that to become revival in the truest sense.

So if what I am saying is true, then we persevere. We remain within the soil and we allow His hands and His will to have their perfect way. We go the distance and we don't easily uproot or replant ourselves because the going gets tough. Be encouraged, friend—you are a vineyard, garden, and harvest field waiting to happen. Take heart, remain, and trust His hands to perfect His will within you. And finally...

Don't forget: "Seeds of greatness" never expire. Unlike natural seeds that do expire, the seeds of greatness within you never will. I got saved at fifteen into a church that was a little obsessed with end-time teaching. For the most part, it was fine, but I was young and naive, so for some (ridiculous) reason I decided to buy and store some seeds, just in case the world went rogue and there was no food to survive. Lord knows what I was thinking—as if I could plant a veggie garden in the middle of the apocalypse. I kept them in my underwear drawer (which is even more hilarious). I think there was also some random speculation that the planets were aligning (hello), and some overseas preacher had prophesied that something catastrophic was happening in the early eighties. Needless to say, we're nearly four decades on and still here.

The hilarious thing was that I stowed my seeds away in the late seventies. One day my boyfriend/fiancé (Brian Charles

Houston) discovered my seeds. Not that he was fossicking in my undies drawer. Perish that thought. But the ridiculous thing is that my seeds had *expired*. Of course they had—everything of this world has an expiry date. Recalling this nonsense, I asked my assistant to Google how long seeds last. She replied, "Well, Pastor Bobbie, some packets last two years and others longer... corn, onion, leek, chives, and parsnips last two years... cabbage, chicory, endive, cucumber, squash, and tomato last six to eight years." Hilarious. I have no memory of what veggies I thought would sustain me until the second coming.

I don't know if that story made you laugh, cry, or go check the date on your seeds! In all truthfulness, we don't need to fear this world or how the events of the future will play out. We have every reason to be wise, observant of the times, and always maturing in our ability to listen to God's direction, but the tenor of Scripture teaches us that our heavenly Father is well able to watch over His own in troublesome times. There is plenty of promise and stories to that end in the Bible. One such story is found in 1 Kings 17, where a series of miraculous provisions watched over the prophet Elijah, including ravens bringing him food at one point. If God can do it for Elijah, He can certainly do it for you and me—just don't shoot the raven with the bag of groceries out of the air! Lightheartedness aside, I have been heard to say that the safest place to be in this world is bang smack in the middle of God's will for your life.

However, what we do need to be mindful of is the *untapped and uncultivated potential within the soil of our own heart*. Again, you are a vineyard, garden, and beautiful field waiting to happen. Allow God to plant and nurture you to fruitfulness. Allow Him to tend the potential within to full expression, and forever stay within the soil of His purpose. None of us graduate from stirring up the gift or calling within, and there is not a day or stretching new opportunity where I do not remind myself to do that.

Never underestimate the labor of your life. The woman who spoke over my life at that campsite meeting all those years ago acknowledged a willingness to plow up hard ground and pave a way. At the time, I had a limited insight of what that might mean in the years ahead. All I knew to do, alongside my husband, was be faithful with what was in our hands. God entrusted a congregation and a nation—and for the past thirty years we have simply sought to give our best and finest to both. I want to encourage you to do likewise. Be faithful in and with the soil of your life and planting.

This book is about navigating the challenges and wonder of life, love, and leadership. None of this is truly achievable without revelation that a *divine exchange* exists and is within your reach—so come with me as I share a handful of defining moments experienced on this remarkable, and yet crazy, pilgrimage home.

SEVEN

STAY WITHIN THE
DIVINE EXCHANGE
(The Waiting)

I honestly didn't know whether to shout hallelujah…*or vomit!*

My husband and two dear friends sat quietly in the dimly lit ambiance of our small apartment in California. It had been a fabulous and yet demanding season of busyness. We'd been on tour throughout the United States, had been darting back and forth across that big blue pond called the Pacific (to navigate our world in Australia), and I was in the middle of completing *The Sisterhood* book together with the madness of landing the creative threads of our pending twentieth year of Colour Conference.

A month or so earlier, Brian and I had agreed to a relaxed dinner with friends who live in Los Angeles. They were keen for us to connect with another couple by the name of Matt and

Laurie Crouch, who run the Trinity Broadcasting Network. It was during that dinner, as the girls talked furiously and passionately at one end of the table (yes, my Greek, highly talkative friend Christine may have been there), that Matt quietly leaned over to Brian and asked if he had ever considered a channel. For nearly three decades Brian's teaching (including our worship and music) had been aired in 180 nations around the world, so I'm sure Brian's mind was processing the question within that framework. Then, in almost the same sentence as the question, Matt leaned in further and presented an opportunity that was completely unexpected. He more or less offered Brian . . . *an entire television channel*! Not just a segment or a better time slot but an entire independent channel within the TBN family—a channel with the capacity to reach into the homes of literally multiplied millions around the world, and a channel that we would have complete freedom to rebrand as Hillsong.

It was in this context that we sat in our little one-bedroom apartment a few weeks later. Brian, with two of our dear colleagues, had just come back from a second meeting, and from what they could fathom, the offer was genuine and definitely on the table.

To say the least, *God* had opened a miraculous and surprising door. Each February we launch the coming year with what we call Vision Sunday. Amid whatever vision is unfolding as a global house, there is always language that seems to prophetically frame our endeavors. The language of the surrounding years had been *"pioneer again," "unusual miracles,"* and *"new roads, new rivers."* In what felt like a split-second, unanticipated, and almost undreamed-of way, God was setting us up to pioneer again in fields we had never imagined. He was unleashing an undeniable and unusual miracle, because (hello) it's not every day you go to dinner and walk out with a TV channel, nor is it every day that a couple you barely know offers an opportunity to build upon a legacy paved by them, their parents, and others. And more than anything, God was propelling us onto a *stretching new road* that would require serious new faith and new rivers of provision.

A television channel had fallen out of the sky and into our laps, with an opportunity to create twenty-four-hour television content and take the message and testimony (so dear to our heart) to an expansive audience around the world. Hence the quietness in my lounge room, hence our faces being a paler shade of our normal selves (marginal shock), and hence my inner reaction: "Lord, I honestly don't know whether to shout hallelujah or throw up." And in all truthfulness, I think I wanted to do the latter.

I share this story because these pathways forward are an endless journey of new horizons that are going to excite, exhilarate, and cause you to stand in awe of His grace—but they are also *horizons of opportunity* that will freak the living daylights out of you at times, and invariably stretch you, not just out of your comfort zone but out of your very birthday suit too. They're horizons that will put demands on your capacity and cause you to dig deep in order to not abandon the idea for fear of inadequacy and inability to deliver. Horizons that will test your faith and cause you to discover a deep and flowing well within, and an even deeper and overflowing supply from above.

Now, you might be wired somewhat differently from me. The thought of such an opportunity might incite nothing but the "Hallelujah Chorus" (on repeat) within you, but for me personally, the thought of our church running and producing a television channel was daunting. Not because I'm afraid of new territory, or because I wasn't aware that indeed an anointed team would step up to the plate. I've lived my entire adult life taking on new territory—I know God is always faithful and I am not unfamiliar with the stretch needed for any degree of expansion—but the daunting aspect was the reality of our already massive, busy, and demanding ministry. In a world where we often joke that there are not enough months in the year (let alone hours in the day or days in the week), all I could process was "How on earth are we going to add yet another enormous layer to our already ridiculous lives? How is our already stretched and ever-willing team going to facilitate the demands that come with such an amazing and God-entrusted new door? And (hello) we're a church, not a TV channel!"

As an aside for those who are leaders, I know that part of my initial panic was simply a pastoral heart that leaps to protect *the distinctives* of our house that have never been compromised—distinctives that have attracted and maintained the anointing of God upon our church. Because let's face it, when a new door opens, when the pace suddenly accelerates, and when some team players are forced to run before they've even walked, it's really easy to lose precious core (gold) values to seemingly good but nevertheless brass values.

If you are unfamiliar with gold and brass values, let me try to explain. A gold value is a core belief. It resonates with true intent and heart. It's pure, unadulterated, and weighty. A brass value is almost indistinguishable to someone who doesn't truly understand the difference. It's close to truth, but it is actually a clanging cymbal. The Apostle Paul captures the difference: "If I speak in the tongues of men or of angels, but do not have love, I am only a resounding gong or a clanging cymbal" (1 Cor. 13:1 NIV). In other words, you can have all the religious rhetoric in the world, but if you don't exemplify love, it all rings shallow and untrue. You can have the appearance of something noble and weighty, but in reality it is presenting as something less than noble.

A classic example is the biblical principle of generosity. We honor God with our finances and sow in order that God will open the windows of heaven and pour out such blessing that we can be an effective blessing to others (see Mal. 3). Every healthy church knows the truth within this eternal principle. Yet the brass value is "give in order to get." Often that shallow brass value is all a secular or cynical world can see, yet the gold value is that we all need to increase in order that we can make a difference in the world.

Another example would be the ministry platform. The spotlight is often upon individuals because (gold value) the spotlight allows more to hear and be exposed to the good news. The brass (tarnished) version is when people are seduced by the spotlight (or limelight) and begin believing it is all about them and their gift. We allowed a Hollywood-produced movie (*Hillsong: Let Hope Rise*, released in 2016) to be made about our church, not because we wanted fame, fortune, or (brass value) exposure. We agreed because it was a gold-value opportunity to share our faith and champion the cause of local churches everywhere. We genuinely wanted to inspire believers, pastors, and churches (including worship and creative teams) within their own local context. The brass-value perception would be: "Look at us, aren't we amazing!…Millions sing our songs…You should all become Hillsong." The movie was produced by others and was even directed by someone who was not a believer as such—and while it was a total joy and honor to be a part of this, we also held initial concerns that our true heart could be distorted into a brass-value experience.

Okay, back to the subject of *the stretch* and those moments when you feel like you are incapable of delivering the goods.

Well, friend, in the natural we can't. Gift, talent, enthusiasm, passion, due diligence, willingness, hard work, and even remarkable "capacity" can carry us all so far, but there are going to be moments along the path when we realize that our own strength has serious limitations. We are going to find ourselves in situations where we discover the power of what many call "the divine exchange": that moment of truth where you know your own strength and capacity are exhausted, and the only alternative is to look up and engage strength from a different realm. It's an exchange that is more than mere provision (or supply for the vision). It's something deeper that pulls a person to their knees, desperate and poured out. It's something that carries a vulnerability about it that is neither wrong nor bad but simply needful—a beautiful vulnerability that brings you to a place of humility wherein you surrender and exchange "your all" for His, a vulnerability where you discover how wonderful God is and how present His Spirit is to help. So if my journey could teach you anything, I would say...

WISDOM AND TRUTH ARE LEARNED ON THE ROAD

I honestly believe that this kingdom road we are all navigating will never *disappoint, fail, or destroy* you. If we could hear the ancients from heaven right now (even those martyred for their faith), they'd be adding a hearty "Amen!" Again, it is the road that teaches us the actual and costly wisdom spoken of in Proverbs 5, which then becomes *costly and outworked wisdom for others.* If you never step out or if you suddenly hesitate for fear of what lies ahead, you negate the journey's ability to teach you the many-layered revelations that God has assigned you to learn. And by way of definition, revelation is simply "revealed truth."

I also believe wisdom is costly—costly because it has cost someone something to unearth and absorb it, and costly perhaps because an ocean of blood, sweat, and tears was shed in the process. This is where we live in such a privileged age: People share sermons or write books about their *costly experience,* and if you and I have enough insight to perceive what they are saying, we can glean from their costly experience and possibly save ourselves a few trips around the proverbial mountain or a trip too close to hell. Pastors and teachers who labor weekly to bring life-changing sermons, authors who labor to create perfect words, and songwriters and musicians (and all faith-inspired artisans, for that matter) who give all to marry lyric, melody, and truth, do so in order that those along the pathway get it right. They do it so there are words and testimony to refer to and songs to sing as we travel forward. Revelation 12 says that the saints overcame by the blood of the Lamb and *the word of their testimony* (see Rev. 12:11). Today we get that testimony in so many mediums.

When it comes to what is learned only on the road, I would remind you that *heightened calling* often presents *heightened territory,* which sometimes presents *heightened aggravation* from all that opposes the kingdom, which is why the foundations of our faith, thinking, and convictions need to be secure. Favor and blessing are wonderful, and who doesn't love an open door like I just wrote of (the TV channel)? But trust me: You cannot effectively pioneer new territory without the spiritual stakes changing. People often observe Hillsong and think that everything our church touches just turns to gold with the wave of a wand. I do believe an uncanny favor rests upon our house for kingdom purpose, but every inch of advancing the kingdom—of pioneering new ground, of persevering, of not drawing back, of resisting mediocrity, of building a church that has not diminished with years, of planting vibrant churches around the world and creating a song for the Body of Christ to sing—has come with some kind of *heat, opposition, attack, or fire.* Every step! And it's in those very steps that we have had our moments of divine exchange.

Allow me to encourage you that the road you find yourself upon has *your steps ordered by the Lord* (see Ps. 37:23). As I have said in previous chapters, Jesus goes before you, He is alongside, and He is your trustworthy rear guard when needed. His exchange of grace (Grace, Grace) is ever ready and waiting for you. But the miracle is in the waiting. Therefore, don't forget:

EVEN YOUNG MEN FAINT AND NEED TO WAIT

In fact, on that note, we all need to wait.

No one is exactly sure how old David was when he wrote the 27th Psalm. Theologians debate his age, but however old he was, he had a living revelation of what it was to "wait." In the psalm, he reveals that the Lord is his light and salvation and the faithful stronghold of his life. He demonstrates a vivid understanding of the safety and surety that is found within the House of God and His presence. The psalm speaks of troublesome times, enemies and siege, and of separation from the security of family, yet the secret of David's life is shown in the final verses: "I remain confident of this: I will see the goodness of the LORD in the land of the living. *Wait for the* LORD; be strong and take heart and wait for the LORD" (Ps. 27:13–14 NIV; emphasis mine). In the margin of my current Bible, I have drawn a heart around these verses and written the words "wait, wait, wait."

Our ability to wait on God is imperative. Isaiah 40 is magnificent on this subject also. It opens in verse 1 with the relentless caring heart of God: "Comfort, comfort My people, says your God." It ends with powerful words relating to the divine exchange:

> He gives power to the faint and weary, and to him who has no might He increases strength [causing it to multiply and making it to abound]. Even youths shall faint and be weary, and [selected] young men shall feebly stumble and fall exhausted; *but those who wait for the Lord* [who expect, look for, and hope in Him] shall change and renew their strength and power; they shall lift their wings and mount up [close to God] as eagles [mount up to the sun]; they shall run and not be weary, they shall walk and not faint or become tired. (Isaiah 40:29–31 AMPC; emphasis mine)

The church is coming of age generationally, with more and more younger people in the mix of ministry and kingdom endeavor, but youthfulness alone doesn't make you immune from the lessons within these verses. In fact, more than the older guard (who have had a lifetime to figure this), the young men and women of today need someone to tell them that they are not invincible and that they also need to learn the patient art of waiting and the ebb and flow of a life given to serving Christ.

Our ministry is overflowing with awesome, gifted, talented (and kick-butt brilliant) young people. We are not alone in this—ministries of similar spirit around the world are exactly the same: They are full of young people who are *wired and anointed* for the generation they find themselves alive in and called to. They are often standing and building on the shoulders of those who took years to create the platforms they've been entrusted with, platforms that are often exponential because of the digital and connected world we now live in. In so many ways, the world is their oyster and there is no end of opportunity. Yet Scripture is clear: "Even youths shall faint and be weary, and [*selected*] young men shall feebly stumble and fall exhausted," so if experience could teach you anything, I would say . . .

Wasted strength and spent strength are different. To all the "select" young men and women and to all the "still select" older men and women: What is a waste of strength as opposed to a proactive spending of strength?

Fighting the wrong battles and allowing your energy to be sapped by responses or things that achieve nothing (or take you nowhere) is the difference. Psalm 90:12 reminds us to number our days in order not to waste them—the intent that we gain a heart of wisdom from each and every day, each and every challenge, and each and every opportunity to respond correctly, or not. I want to encourage you to "spend your energy" wisely on proactive responses that are going to yield something positive (as in vintage pressed fruit, and not sour). Learn to govern and steward your responses.

When our son Ben and daughter-in-law Lucille felt the call to the west coast of America, they of course had to begin the (daunting) process of visa application. They were so excited to be planting and pioneering Hillsong Los Angeles. Everything was in perfect motion, and then a small glitch meant they needed to return to Sydney for the visa process to continue. The church plant in LA was already in motion, with those on the ground carrying the early stages of this new room. Ben, Luc, and their three little girls moved back into our family home in Sydney, because their belongings had already been packed away. The challenge was that the visa clearance became prolonged. Anyone who has ever migrated or applied for a visa to another nation knows that you can't rush or force the system—so my kids found themselves squished and stuck for eight weeks in the back bedroom of their parents' house in the back burbs of Sydney, when all they wanted was the City of Angels and the excitement of the new plant there.

Brian and I came home from overseas at that time, and to be honest, I found my gorgeous daughter-in-law in a slight state of (understandable) exasperation. She desperately wanted to be somewhere else, and here they were, in the visa waiting game. Lucille hopefully won't mind me saying, but I remember going into mother mode. I said something like, "Honey, listen to me, it's out of your hands...you can't do anything...being exasperated will achieve nothing...so *spend* your energy in this not-fabulous season proactively."

The same week, another layer in one of the spiritual battles we've fought in Australia heightened. I remember saying to our church, "Guys, it's no use any of us *wasting strength*, exasperated by the unfairness of all this... We have to arrest our proactive energy and begin to *pray* and fight the spiritual forces that are camping in and around the greater issue."

Stuff happens in life. Sometimes what should be amazing and perfect turns into a dog's breakfast of what shouldn't be. Life isn't always smooth sailing or fair, and it's so easy to fall into the trap of despondency, negativity, and passivity. So much proactive faith-energy gets wasted, which is exactly what the enemy wants. Better to arrest your thinking, arrest your spirit, arrest your faith, and turn the flow of energy in the opposite direction.

Being spent is not life-threatening. Honestly... it may feel like it is, but take it from me—it isn't. Being (or feeling) spent is occasion to experience the divine exchange this chapter is devoted to. It's opportunity for an infusion of strength from above. When you are poured out, that is exactly when He pours in. Did you hear that? In fact, we are supposed to arrive in heaven somewhat spent. This is the nature of the Great Commission: to go into the world and give all in the same way Jesus gave all. However, the good news for us is that we don't die in the pouring out. He did the dying. Instead we discover a God whose burden is light and whose yoke is easy, and that in the pouring out, there is room for replenishment. The spirit of servanthood is simply that we are willing to take up our cross, if need be.

Allow me to remind you again of Isaiah 40. The promise is that He gives power to the faint and weary, and to him who has exhausted his might He increases strength, causing it to miraculously abound—but the secret of His comfort is in the waiting. "*Comfort, comfort My people.*" We serve a good God who is not trying to kill us—He wants you to know comfort, kindness, and welfare in the midst of pouring out your life for Him. Poured out, yes. Dead, no!

There have been several occasions along this journey where I have discovered that spent is not life-threatening but rather an occasion to discover something marvelous. One was in a moment that felt like a personal altar call, one was learned in the field, one in the battle, and one watching my own children. So again, if my experience can create perspective for you...

Find strength in the surrender. The definition of surrender is to "cease resistance, give up, or hand over." There was nothing within me wanting to give up in a negative sense, but I felt completely poured out. It was a Sunday night, and as a multi-campus church we had gathered under one roof in Sydney's largest indoor venue for the recording of our live worship album *This Is Our God* (2008). Back in that season, we recorded in March, and this particular year we back-ended the recording into the same weekend (and venue) as the Colour Conference (which creates, as you can imagine, a unique demand on everyone behind the scenes). Colour had been truly amazing, beautiful, and perfect— women had gathered from far and wide and had leant into the deeper mandate taking shape within the Sisterhood.

Unlike the three days prior, when I had been down the front, hosting and running the conference, Brian and I got to sit up the very back of the venue for the recording—"up in the gods" as they say, where you have a bird's-eye view of everything and possibly suffer vertigo. As the night unfolded and as we all worshipped like there was no tomorrow, my son Joel and the team began singing "With Everything." If you don't know the song, the lyrics are timeless and honestly capture who we are as a church…a bunch of Jesus followers who are completely humbled to be part of His story unfolding on the earth. Allow me to include the lyrics to give perspective to what was happening:

Open our eyes to see the things
That make Your heart cry,
To be the church that You would desire,
Light to be seen.
Break down our pride and all the walls
We've built up inside.
Our earthly crowns and all our desires
We lay at Your feet.
So let hope rise and darkness tremble
In Your holy light,
That every eye will see Jesus, our God,
Great and mighty to be praised.
God of all days, Glorious in all of Your ways.
The majesty, the wonder and grace,
In the light of Your name.
With everything, with everything,
We will shout for your glory.
With everything, with everything,
We will shout forth your praise.
Our hearts they cry, Be glorified,
Be lifted high, above all names.
For You our King,
With everything,
We will shout forth your praise.

—"WITH EVERYTHING," WORDS AND
MUSIC BY JOEL HOUSTON, 2008

As song, sound, and passion for this glorious King began to fill every corner and crevice of that stadium, the presence of God drew near like nothing I've ever experienced. With arms fully outstretched, I remember worshipping literally on tiptoes, as if being two inches taller would bring me closer to this God who had invaded the room. The entire stadium was in a stance of surrender, not least my own son, who told me that in this season he felt "the most crushed"—and yet it was also in this season that God birthed the call to New York so clearly within him.

As the song built to where we sing "With everything, with everything," I could barely breathe. I was in utter abandonment, and yet my worship still felt so inadequate in light of who He truly is. Have you ever felt like that? I felt like I had poured out everything I had for the girls, for the conference, for the cause. I felt creatively spent. My inner cry was, "*God*, I don't know how to keep telling this story…*God*, I don't know how it can be more beautiful than it just was…Father, I am at the end of what I have." So as we sang "With everything, with everything, with everything," that song became an altar of surrender to His power, genius, and creativity for the future. It became a moment of divine enabling that has allowed me to continue and stay the path of this now global women's movement. Fast-track another decade and people still say, "Bobbie, that was the best conference yet!" The comment always makes me smile because I feel that every year was the best, simply because we gave our best—yet, as we are constantly learning, heaven is an endless supply of wonder and shall continue to be so until that perfect day.

Friend, I don't know how this story will resonate with you.

Perhaps you are at your "creative end" of knowing how to reach your family, build that business, or pastor your church. I want to encourage you that in that place of being spent and exhausted, God has provision for you. There is more I could say of that night and season, but suffice to say, God is immeasurably faithful as we surrender and discover that He is an endless flow within.

Find strength in the field. This memory is vivid. I was in Kiev (Ukraine) hosting the women's conference there. That year we held two conferences, back-to-back. The first three-day conference ended at 5:00 p.m. and the second three-day conference started at 7:30 p.m. (two and half hours later). I had one hour to race back to the hotel, quickly shower, and return to the venue. The traffic was manic in downtown Kiev. I remember walking down the long corridor of the old and yet grand hotel we were staying in (love it when your room is a mile from the foyer). I turned the key, walked in, and suddenly the reality of it all overwhelmed me.

I don't know if you've ever hosted anything of magnitude. The physical workload is one thing, but the spiritual weight of carrying such an event is huge, especially in a foreign (former Soviet) land that has historically denied or not shown empathy toward the value and worth of their women. The Kiev conference carries an added demand for me personally, because everything needs translation into Russian, not only the teaching but also the hosting and the way the entire gathering is woven together.

When I frantically stepped into the shower, I momentarily succumbed. All I could utter inside my heart was, "God, I can't do this...I'm so tired...I can't do this." Yet, friend, as I chose to stir up every gift and measure within, as I began to choose praise over defeat and declare that I can do all things through Christ who strengthens me, something happened. As I stepped out of that shower, a sudden infusion of supernatural strength met me. I'm not sure I had ever experienced it quite as tangibly. I raced back to the venue, walked into the greenroom area, and quite honestly it felt like I wasn't at the end of the Colour marathon that year, but at the beginning. And remarkably, God did a similar thing for those sharing the weight of the conference back at the venue. Our lead pastors there had dimmed the lights in the room, stilled their hearts, and rested for thirty minutes—and in the resting they found renewal.

The divine exchange is not the domain of an exclusive few. I discovered His enabling in the field. I was doing what I was called to do, and amid the pace, He met me there. In the same way, He will meet you as you keep your hand to the plow and your eyes on the task at hand.

Find strength in the battle. If you get a chance, listen to my husband's message called "Troubling the Troubler" about the thirty-one kings that Joshua had to defeat before the children of Israel could fully enter the promised land. Sometimes there are strongholds to overcome before you see the promise materialize—and sometimes the battle feels long and drawn out, but if you persevere you will conquer what needs to be conquered. It was in this context that the following divine exchange happened.

The battle for our nation felt fierce that day. Brian and I had flown in from Europe. We landed running and had gone hard for the next two days. I woke up on the Friday morning tired and unwell—and very mindful of what was pending in the coming week regarding a Royal Commission (an Australian commission to inquire into and find systems of response to abuses that tragically happen in various institutions in society, including some corners of the church). Brian was contributing to the inquiry in context of his father's failings, but he was facing media frenzy because of the profile of our church. It would be untrue to say I was overwhelmed, but I had never felt as spiritually exposed and vulnerable as I did that day. The reality of sexual abuse is inexcusable at any level of society, and as a local church we are active advocates against it, but in this instance, it felt like other agendas were at play. It felt like the forces of hell were gathering and circling against the integrity of a church and a reputation that is good and upright and which always seeks to do what is right. It felt like a dark enemy was surrounding us with the intent to defame and destroy. So I did what I know to do…I waited. *I waited and prayed.* I waited for my Lord to bring relief to my weighted-down heart. Lunchtime came. Still waiting. I needed to get out and find a distraction, so I went for a manicure, pedicure, and massage. Yep, that's what you do, gentlemen—when it's all proving too much, take a lesson from the Sisterhood and go for a mani-pedi. (I'm being humorous, if only to soften the intensity of what I'm sharing.)

To be honest, I lingered at the nail bar because I couldn't face going home and being alone. I felt assailed by darkness. At 4:30 p.m., the wait ended. In my bathroom, as I leant in to apply makeup for what was Friday night church, it was as if a breath of supernatural strength entered the room. It literally infused my entire body, soul, and spirit. Have you ever seen one of those tall, fabric, promotional "air men" outside a car dealership (the ones that billow and bend uncontrollably)? Well, that's how I felt. I felt weakened and vulnerable . . . but because I waited, He came. His Spirit came and infused my soul for the challenge ahead. I walked out of that bathroom and into church that evening feeling empowered. I knew He would not fail, because it's impossible for God to fail, yet it's in these moments of waiting that you discover the one who is truly your personal Savior and King.

I add an important footnote here. How many precious people have ended their wait in the bathroom, but in a tragic way? How many have felt such hopelessness that the only way out is to take their own life? I exhort you to discover the "beautiful exchange" that is found only in Christ. In doing so, you may well rescue not only yourself but another from a fate you and they were never created to experience. I know a girl who woke up one day hating all that her life represented. She didn't know what to do, but her parents had instilled enough heritage for her to know that Christian music might help. Naively she Googled "Christian music" and the first song she encountered was titled "Beautiful Exchange." In that moment, the Spirit led her to a church, wherein she dedicated her life to Jesus. Never doubt that your divine exchange may well become the thread of saving grace for another.

Find strength observing others. And finally, the fourth moment I share is watching my offspring—my own son and those he does life with. It was during the recording of the Hillsong movie, which I have briefly mentioned. The culmination of weeks of cameras following them across several continents came in the LA Forum, a theater seating over 17,000.

If you've seen the film you will understand the tensions of the night. Not for lack of due diligence, the entire team were fighting the deadline and the discomfort of "lights, cameras, action." The boys were still perfecting everything (as in, everything!) during setup and rehearsals. In the eleventh hour, e-mails were still flying to and from Australia to those who ensure the lyrics are theologically correct, and multimedia for the screens was still being created (let alone tested) as the crowds lined up outside. Jad, who sees himself as an armor-bearer to Joel, sang one song ("Empires") in blind faith because it was still unfinished minutes before the event began. When he stepped up to the microphone in front of thousands and with cameras in all directions, it was the *first time* all the elements of music, words, and production had come together for that particular song.

As a church, we had been extended an amazing opportunity with this movie. It tracked the creation of a new album and, more important, told the story of our church through the lens of the band. However, to execute and deliver this project, amid all the pressures of an already huge schedule and church life, meant the film came with its fair share of drama. Joel was leading the crew in deadlines that were literally squeezing the vine. They were exhausted. They had been away from family and home for weeks on end, and the pressures on the night were extreme, mostly because this wasn't merely a music doc about a rock group. This was about conceiving and birthing songs for "the church" to sing—songs that reflect, honor, and echo the living, timeless, and holy Word of God. With something as weighty as that, you can't snap your fingers at God and demand the "God-drop" just because a deadline demands it. Waiting on heaven while working within earthly deadlines is one of the great tensions of anyone stewarding opportunities like this.

I wasn't present in the evening because of a former commitment that I didn't want to break. It killed me not to be there, mostly to support my son. A few days earlier (as we closed the Hillsong Conference in New York), he had called across the room and motioned me to pray. He doesn't often ask his mom to pray. I knew what he was saying—they were spent, exhausted, and walking on a razor-thin faith edge.

That night, when the prayer meeting was called, I heard that Jason (beloved friend, son, and tour manager) came to get Joel from his room. It was time to go. Joel was still working on lyrics (I birthed an avatar and a perfectionist!). He closed his laptop and they walked down the hall. The film captures the moment; it captures the tension on his face, but I am not sure everyone will perceive the pain being felt in that corridor. In the prayer meeting, they gathered to link shoulders and pray. Our worship teams always pray. Brian was there, as well as Cass (Langton), who oversees our creative community.

I heard that in that prayer meeting, vulnerability was at an all-time high. I heard that as they bent knee and heart heavenward, "select young men" may have wept and dissolved into tears in that back room. Not for wrong reasons, but for right reasons—tears that come when you are poured out, when you want to fall exhausted (as Isaiah prophesied), and yet you know that to rise in faith is what the journey requires. I heard also that in that moment, a certain select young man (my firstborn) lowered his head and broke. I heard that with strained and weary voice, he whispered, "I've got nothing, I've got nothing."

I have a picture from that night. Found it on social media.

It's of Joel standing onstage in the spotlight as the night began. I don't see the spotlight or fame or wonder. All I see is my son (and the members of Hillsong UNITED, who I love as my own) stepping out into the divine exchange. That night they stepped out not into an earthly spotlight but into the light of the Father, Son, and Spirit... that night *they drew on the unfailing, unending, immeasurable, perfect, and faithful strength of God.* Why? So that others might experience the very same presence and grace of God in and through that film.

That night they waited upon the Lord, they renewed their strength, they mounted up as eagles mount up to the sun... and they ran with the anointing and calling of Christ upon their lives. I can't tell you how proud of them I am. I hope I've done their moment of divine exchange justice. If not, they'll correct me (kids do that) or tell of it themselves in their own literary works one day. All I know is that Brian and I stand in awe of the devotion of those around us—the many thousands whose stories I haven't included yet who equally give all for the glory and expansion of God's great love.

Needless to say, there is a place of exchange where we can renew our strength. I opened this chapter by telling you of certain new territory that came with the temptation, on my part, to throw up. A few months later, driving away from our makeshift TV studio, I had a moment in my car where I felt God whisper, "Bobbie, you know there is an anointing within all of this for you." In other words, He was reassuring my little heart (yet again) that there is always grace within any assignment He entrusts. To be anointed simply means "to be smeared with ability." Amid the willingness to say yes, amid the hard work and labor, amid the pressures and tensions, there is always a God who wants to smear you with ability and grace to deliver.

As I wrote in *The Sisterhood*, there is a scarlet thread of redemption that wraps itself around our hearts and anchors us to the very Son of God, who sits with His Father in the throne room of heaven. They intercede and watch over us from above. You are not alone in what you do. Heaven's endless supply waits for you. I encourage you also to wait and receive.

EIGHT

STAY IN THE FIELD

(Eyes Wide Open)

D arling, are you awake?"

"Yes," he replied. Then suddenly he pulled the car to a halt and said, "You need to drive. I just answered you, but I was asleep." With that, he got out of the car, leaving me to scramble across the middle console. As my tall and capable husband climbed into the passenger side, all I could see in the rear-vision mirror were giant headlights bearing down from behind. We were stopped in the middle of the highway, somewhere between Liverpool and Birmingham, with a monster truck about to rear-end us if I didn't shake a leg and get the car moving.

My husband isn't in the habit of doing such random things. He's actually a very good driver—probably somewhat calmer these days than in his wild youth—and I usually feel very safe in his hands. The reason he had fallen asleep for a microsleep nanosecond is because he was fiercely jet-lagged. We had flown from Sydney to England via New York for a four-week ministry trip. Being young and minus our kids, we had gone hard for two days in the big bustling excitement of the Big Apple. We didn't have much to our name back in those days, but my darling bought me a beautiful deep-red coat at Bloomingdale's that I (embarrassingly) may have worn 24/7 (even inside houses) for the entire four weeks that we were away. English temps were not what this Aussie girl was used to. After we landed in London, we got ourselves to Liverpool in the north, and then Brian spoke at a youth rally that night in Birmingham. This was back in the day when my man was the popular and often sought-out youth ministry speaker. The only problem was that he literally hadn't slept since leaving Sydney. He'd been awake for days. How he managed to preach his soul out to those English kids and be conscious and upright is a mystery. Little wonder he fell asleep as we hit the road back to Liverpool. I must have sensed his weariness, hence the question. I thought he was awake—he sounded awake when I spoke to him, and he answered me as if he was awake—but he was asleep.

A perfect example of the world we inhabit and, sadly, of some corners of the Body of Christ. All appearances say "wide awake" yet so many are in fact asleep at the wheel. They're asleep to who they really are in Christ, asleep to what's going on in and around them, and tragically often asleep to the dangers bearing down on the road, like the giant truck with headlights on full beam. What is at stake is not a mere nanosecond in time, but often a lifetime of existence, including the lives of others. Isaiah doesn't mince words. He says of the holy city (which is a picture of our hearts and the church at the culmination of time): "*Wake up, wake up!* Pull on your boots, Zion! Dress up in your Sunday best, Jerusalem, holy city!...Brush off the dust and get to your feet, captive Jerusalem! Throw off your chains, captive daughter of Zion!" (Isa. 52:1–2 MSG; emphasis mine).

We have a world in need of triage, a harvest in need of tendering, and a church around the world that needs to be more awake than ever, so if my (stay the path) journey could teach you anything, I would say...

STAND TALL AND LET HIM LOVE YOU

Allow me to quote a scene from a novel called *The Book of God* by Walter Wangerin. It's a beautiful read that brings to life the pilgrimage of God's people through the history of the Bible. What captivated my heart was where the author writes of Isaac and Rebekah. The servant of Abraham had gone in search of a bride for his son, Isaac:

In the month that followed, Rebekah and the old servant traveled from her home in Paddan-aram on the same road Abraham himself had taken more than sixty-five years earlier, a long southward route. They crossed the Jordan River at Succoth and journeyed yet farther south than the Salt Sea into the Negev. On the evening of the thirtieth day, while the camels were moving with weary languor, Rebekah lifted her eyes and saw a man strolling alone across the fields, his head bent down in meditation. "Who is that?" she said. She alighted from her camel and went to the old servant of Abraham. "Do you see that man in the distance?" she asked. "Who is he?" "Ah, that's the son of my master. That is Isaac." So Rebekah covered her face with a veil and waited to be seen by the man who would be her husband. In the Negev, then, Isaac took Rebekah to his tent, and she became his wife, and he loved her completely. He never loved another as long as he lived. He said, "As soon as I saw the woman standing tall by the side of a white field, I fell in love with her." He was forty years old.

As soon as he saw the woman *standing tall by the side of a white field, he fell in love with her*. Friend, when I read those words my heart nearly stopped, for surely that is how our God sees us. The fields are white unto harvest and His deepest desire is that we enter those fields as fellow laborers. And when we do...His heart will well with love and gratitude.

Abraham and Isaac paint for us a picture of our heavenly Father and Son. Study the moment for yourself in Genesis 22. A sacrifice of atonement was required and Abraham was prepared to offer his very own and much-awaited son. It was a stunning test of devotion—thank God that we now live in a new covenant of grace. In the eleventh hour, God of course stepped in, providing a substitute animal for sacrifice, but what was being exampled was willingness and surrender, on Abraham's part, and uncontained faithfulness on God's part. Because, as history reveals, God did give His only begotten Son for the atonement of sin and our ongoing redemption (see John 3:16). The Old Testament account is full of wisdom and gold, and the lesson is beautiful. Therefore:

FIND YOUR STATURE

My prayer for you is that you will find your stature also in and alongside those fields. God doesn't want his children bent over and struggling, or being blown in all directions like the bendy plastic "air men" I spoke of in the previous chapter. Find your personal rise-up moments and stand tall. On the scale of eternity, it doesn't matter if you get knocked down in life—the important thing is to get up again. It's never pleasant, but you are not the first person to experience the hard knocks of life, and you won't be the last. If the fall has winded you, I empathize (I really do), but re-catch your breath and stand up.

I remember playing with the neighborhood kids when I was a little girl. We were chasing each other around the perimeter of the house. As I took the corner at great speed (yes, back in the day, when I could run like the wind), the lush green grass was damp underfoot, and down I went on my tailbone. The pain was excruciating, and I carried the injury for a lot of years thereafter. Point is, bends and curves (and damp slippery grass) can take their toll, but as the saying goes, "It ain't over 'til the fat lady sings" (haven't said that for years, and not sure it's politically correct anymore, but nevertheless, if the lungs of a large lady or the trumpet of some large angel aren't sounding—the journey isn't over).

Find the strength to pull yourself up, and then get about finding your grace-stature in Him. Get yourself planted, get yourself among like-spirited people who are going to cheer you on, stir up the dreamscape, and let's stand tall where He needs us to stand tall. When Rebekah said yes to leaving her world, traveling, and becoming Isaac's wife, she was by no means perfect or fully developed. She was young, with much to learn, yet Walter Wangerin captures her willingness and potential stature perfectly. I believe Jesus falls in love with us, over and over and over again (regardless of perfection or not), when we choose to position ourselves near or within the needs of this world.

Find your people. It's never too late to realize that we travel better together and that our stories are intrinsically interwoven. Sometimes it's not until we step back and take a wider-angle view that we realize life and relationships are like a giant puzzle taking shape across the years. I've camped on this thought already, but our choices shape that puzzle. The Word is full of examples to glean from—a classic is that of Naomi and Ruth, the famous story of lineage, destiny, and fields that tell their own story. Allow me to take a page from the Brave Women Run in My Family series that I've been walking our Hillsong girls through for several years. God isn't biased when it comes to gender. He created men and women equal and unique, and His purposes are outworked in and through us all. Therefore, if you're a man, please don't switch off because you think this is a "women of the Bible" story. To be honest, the landscape of history, including the relentless buoyancy of the church that rises and keeps rising, is full of *brave men and women, serving and giving all for the kingdom.*

There is no Ruth story without the Naomi story, and vice versa. In the same way, our stories either enhance or hinder one another. The account is found in the book of Ruth. It tells of severe drought pushing a family into a foreign land. The woman's husband and sons die, and she decides to return to her homeland with her bereaved girls. Halfway home, one daughter-in-law decides to turn back, while the other clings to her mother-in-law and echoes the famous words, "Where you go, I will go; and where you stay, I will stay; your people shall be my people, and your God my God" (Ruth 1:16 NHEB). Together they return to the place of Naomi's birth and the story unfolds of a young woman who finds herself in a field—a field wherein lies destiny, a husband, and a pathway into the very lineage of Jesus.

Allow your hearts to be knit. As you read the story (especially in the Message paraphrase) you'll see some powerful principles. The two women were on the road together and their hearts were set on destiny. A strong and binding (generational) warmth and affection was evident. I exhort you to cherish and protect relationships with those younger (or older) in your life. Give honor where honor is due. Genuinely love and respect those advanced in age or further down the road than you, and genuinely love and respect those younger who are following or alongside. The House of God can and should be a stunning example of this. If one thing marks our Hillsong Church, it is this reality. There exists a genuine love and affection for the people we are doing life with. It's unforced and natural and transcends age barriers, and it is something that Brian and I are very mindful to protect and nurture.

Share a strong kingdom work ethic. "One day Ruth, the Moabite foreigner, said to Naomi, 'I'm going to work; I'm going out to glean among the sheaves, following after some harvester who will treat me kindly.' Naomi said, 'Go ahead, dear daughter'" (Ruth 2:2 MSG; emphasis mine).

The daughter committed herself to work in the harvest. She

wasn't content to ride on the sacrifice of those who had gone before. She wasn't content to wait for her mother-in-law to cut more ground, make all the sacrifice, and figure the future.

I opened this book by sharing a personal word about how Brian and I had cut ground, made sacrifice, and paved a way. At the time, the generation our ministry would probably influence the most were still babies or yet to be born. I'm grateful that (by His grace) we've reproduced after our kind, and that we are surrounded with layers of younger people (like Ruth) who are prepared to work, sacrifice, get into the field, and pave the way forward. Brian and I are not putting ourselves out to pasture (at least not this week), but there is a spirit of release within us and within our global church that says, "Go ahead"—go ahead, cut new ground, take the lead, use your initiative, be innovative, speak the language of this glorious gospel in the language of your generation; accomplish more and do mighty exploits for our God. We're not threatened and we're right behind you if you need wisdom, insight, encouragement (or a good kick in the pants if you go off course or get too full of yourself). Joking...*not joking!* What parent wouldn't yank a child back who is curbside to danger or about to fall off a cliff?

Choose the right field. Ruth chose the right field, proved teachable, worked diligently, and *followed in the wake of the harvesters.* Whatever field of career or vocation you choose, attach it to the greater field of God's kingdom, and I promise that the decision to do so will never lead you astray. We are all created for the cause of Christ. Ministry isn't merely within the confines of church walls. We gather to the House of God (our planting) in order to effectively scatter into the marketplace, in order to be a blessing.

As Brian relentlessly teaches: Don't draw a wall of division between your devotional life and your vocational life, because they're supposed to be beautifully interwoven. A healthy devotional life will only empower and enhance your vocational life, and a healthy understanding of why you are alive will automatically attach itself to the vision of "Thy kingdom come," which is felt and outworked in churches all around the world.

There are so many lessons within Ruth and Naomi's story, not least that Ruth's faithfulness brought her notice and reward. "Eventually she ended up in the *part of the field* owned by Boaz" (Ruth 2:3 MSG). She was in the right field, at the right time, being faithful with all the right things—and God caused her life to collide with the desire of her heart. She married the owner and master of the field and found fulfillment not in shallow (brass value) fame or notoriety, but in being faithful. Boaz actually said, "I've heard all about you—heard about the way you treated your mother-in-law after the death of her husband... God reward you well for what you've done" (Ruth 2:11–12 MSG). Feel free to phone, text, or maybe send your mom-in-law some flowers (wink, wink—Esther? Lucille? Pete?). Ruth also listened to the master's advice to remain with his workers until the harvest was complete. Therefore, in all seriousness:

STAY TO THE END AND STAY WITH THE LABORERS

The exhortation of Boaz (who is another example pointing to Jesus) was: "Stick with my workers until my harvesting is finished" (Ruth 2:21 MSG). Pause for a moment and consider the weight within those words. This is far more than a lesson in farming. It takes courage to stay to the end of anything. On the Mount of Olives, the disciples asked Jesus what the end of the age would look like. Not a small question, right? He described various signs of the times, but he encouraged them not to be alarmed or led astray. It wouldn't hurt for you to read it yourself (in Matthew 24), because the Holy Spirit can then quicken it to you as he sees fit. However, he did speak of an increase of lawlessness and the love of many growing cold. Then the Lord says: "But the one who *endures to the end* will be saved. And this gospel of the kingdom will be proclaimed throughout the whole world as a testimony to all nations, and then the end will come" (Matt. 24:13–14 ESV; emphasis mine).

The one who endures to the end! Who truly knows what that end will look like or require of us—but allow me to remove the fear factor. Our comfort as Christians is to remember that the end hinges on the gospel being proclaimed throughout the entire world as a testimony. All we have to do is *remain faithful within the field entrusted*—remain faithful in testimony, faithful with the truth, and faithful with what is in your hand to do. I am not talking about Christians going into hiding with a suitcase of seeds for the last days (smile), I am talking about the followers of Christ being found busy and attentive—living strong to the end, with hearts ever looking to help those who are lost and in need of redemption.

Honestly, if we all just attended faithfully to what is in our hand right now, the testimony of Christ would do its work in this world. It would prepare a way for Christ, it would deny the enemy his pleasure (of killing, destroying, and interfering with the will of God in people's lives), it would water the harvest to maturity, and (listen to me) it would guarantee your eternal safety. Ruth found herself within a field, gleaning and working the harvest. There *was* danger in the field—danger of being led astray, defiled, and raped. But Naomi told her daughter that if she stayed with the master laborers (and the community of people around them) she would be safe. Ruth said, "He also told me, 'Stick with my workers until my harvesting is finished.'" Naomi said to Ruth, "That's wonderful, dear daughter! Do that! You'll be safe in the company of his young women; no danger now of being raped in some stranger's field" (Ruth 2:21–22 MSG).

Therefore, on that note:

Stay at your post. If my journey has any wisdom for this path, it is to remain at your post. These are not days to be dabbling in the wrong fields, or as the Scripture just said, *some stranger's field.* I'm not suggesting that to be in the right field won't require you to use your hazard lights on occasion, but divine protection is present when you are found in the center of His will (see Ps. 91). Remember the lions are chained and harmless as long as you remain in the center of that path.

I'm confident that you have gathered by now that this glorious kingdom is described as *a battle, a race, and a field*—with those within referred to as soldiers, athletes, and hardworking farmers (see 2 Tim. 2). Nature, history, and Bible truth paint endless pictures and instill lessons here. Athletes who abandon the race do not cross the finish line. It's not a case of supreme or competitive athleticism—it's an issue of devotion, heart, and perseverance. Soldiers that pledge allegiance and then abandon the post court serious threat to themselves and those waging the battle. And farmers who do not know how to read the seasons or the dynamics of harvest put the harvest at risk of being spoiled. Therefore, stay at your post—there are plenty of things seeking to displace you. Ecclesiastes 10:4 reminds us to remain calm even when a ruler or boss (or anyone, for that matter) causes offense, tempting us to withdraw or leave. Remember the lessons I have already shared: Life in the kingdom lane can be messy, but once you settle your convictions, nothing can sabotage you upon the pathway.

Stay hungry for souls. Stay within the breaking of heart and soul for this lost and hurting world. The "because factor" of Isaiah 61 will never diminish in importance until the final curtains are drawn on this world. The because factor is the relentless anointing upon us of God's Spirit, which seeks to take Christ to the broken, captive, blind, and lost. The because factor will never rest until this world has heard the gospel of saving grace. If you want insight into my heart on all this, read the latter part of *The Sisterhood*.

Stay true to responsibility. The Proverbs 31 woman has insight for all of us—men and women. She wasn't afraid to consider new fields of endeavor. However, she never did so at the expense of what was already entrusted. In other words, the romance of changing the world can sometimes lead (or seduce) people away from the responsibility of their own home, family, or local planting. God works from the inside out...*heart, family, home, house, planting, neighborhood, town, city, nation, and then world!* When you remain faithful with what is in your hand, it is remarkable how God will entrust the desires of your heart to make a wider and larger impact. Our church and ministry is a living example of this. Not one person who has remained within the core heartbeat convictions of Hillsong's greater ministry has ever lost sight of what is truly important in this context. Home will always remain the prize that is honored and cherished, and we know that there is no lasting global voice or impact if that is ever compromised. As we have remained planted deep within what is important, the branches of our tree have spread far and wide. If my journey could teach you anything, I would put these thoughts at the top of the list.

The pronoun "she" is generic to all, and "she" is how Christ speaks of His church. Proverbs paints it perfectly:

> She considers a [new] field before she buys or accepts it [expanding prudently and not courting neglect of her present duties by assuming other duties]; with her savings [of time and strength] she plants fruitful vines in her vineyard . . . She tastes and sees that her gain from work [with and for God] is good; her lamp goes not out, but it burns on continually through the night [of trouble, privation, or sorrow, warning away fear, doubt, and distrust]. (Proverbs 31:16 and 18 AMPC)

Sleep with your boots on. Remember the verses from the front end of this chapter: *"Wake up, wake up! Pull on your boots, Zion! Dress up in your Sunday best . . . brush off the dust and get to your feet."* So much I could say, yet so little time or space within these pages to fully express it. Spiritually speaking, we must live exactly as Isaiah prophesies . . . prepared and ready to pull on our boots at the whisper of His approach.

A dream is shared in the romantic pages of the Song of

Songs, chapter 5 to be precise. The story is close to my heart and
the essence of all that the Sisterhood represents. The Shulamite
woman's lover approaches, beckoning her to arise and come with
him. The story is a parallel of Christ's lordship. The verses don't
say where he was leading her, but as I see it, his work in the darkness (or field) was not complete, and he was seeking to include
her. She hears him knocking, yet lingers because, already weary
from a day in the vineyards, she has bathed and put herself to
bed. She doesn't want to soil her feet again. He knocks upon the
lattice of her house (and heart) and eventually she rises because
she loves him, but alas, her lover has departed.

For the 2017 Colour invitation, we captured this moment of
beckoning, urgency, and response with an image of bare and soiled
feet walking across white floorboards toward that open door of
invitation—hopefully, the imagery of the (wind word) breeze
moving the sheer curtains captures a willingness to once again
rise from the comfort and cleanliness of where we might dwell,
to enter again the mess and need of what lies outside. I loathe to
read between the lines or suggest things that are not—however,
I do believe these are days where we all need to sleep with one
eye open, an ear attentive to His gentle beckoning, and our
boots either on or nearby.

Human need upon this planet is not subject to our body clock
timing. In other words, just because we've put ourselves to bed
for (hopefully) a good eight hours' sleep doesn't mean that the
enemy has switched off or that the cry of the afflicted is no longer ascending into the ears of God. So if my journey could share
something that is a growing revelation within my own spirit, it
would be:

STAND TALL AND BEND LOW

As a daughter, pastor, and leader within the Body, I am consumed with the thought of the Spirit and the bride being of *one heart, one voice, and one posture* at the end of the age. If you remotely know me, you will know this to be true, because these words are not merely a sermon title or a verse that has somehow become the theme of the hour for Bobbie Houston. They're words that will constantly appear in my writing because of the weight they bear and because they're at the core of who we are as a ministry. Our greatest desire is to example a body of believers who are knit (heart and soul) to God's holy and majestic Spirit—so:

Learn from the priest. I believe God would definitely have us standing tall and upright beside those white fields. However, I also believe there is a breathtaking and fierce *stance of love* to His Spirit that bends low and intercedes deeply for those broken and lost. I sense God would have us understand a deeper level of this passion and what is needful, on our part, if we are to see a world won for Christ.

A few years ago, we found ourselves at the summer retreat of the well-known Holy Trinity Brompton church in London. Four thousand fabulous Anglican brethren converged into the English countryside, to stay in trailers and meet in a giant marquee tent. Brian and I were honored to share, and I thoroughly enjoyed the entire few days. Another invited speaker was a priest from Rome. As I understood, he was the Vatican priest responsible for sharing the Word of God weekly with the Pope. He spoke for possibly ninety minutes one evening and I want to tell you, quite honestly, it was the most riveting and anointed ninety minutes of any speaker I've ever sat under (and for the record, I've listened to some fairly epic teachers and preachers). This humble man spoke of the Holy Spirit and oozed the presence of God. And then he said something that I have never forgotten: "When you encounter brokenness, bend low, weep...and then point them to Jesus."

My own church will attest that I came home deeply impacted by the experience. Romans chapter 8 is often titled "Life in the Spirit" or "Life Through the Spirit." It reveals a Savior who ascended on high and is seated at the right hand of the Father— yet it also reveals a Savior who still intercedes for us regardless of the victory (verse 34). I find it remarkable that Jesus (even right now as you read these words) is still laboring and interceding for us. In the same way, it says that the Spirit also intercedes for us: "Likewise the Spirit helps us in our weakness. For we do not know what to pray for as we ought, but the Spirit himself intercedes for us with groanings too deep for words" (Rom. 8:26 ESV).

Ponder those words, allow them to sink deep—the Spirit Himself intercedes for you with groaning too deep for words. That basically means we have connection with a God *whose love and longing for the human soul is so deep that words cannot be found worthy of expression.*

Our tears matter. Our concern for the human race matters. If we, as the bride of Christ, are going to be aligned in posture with God's holy and magnificent Spirit in these final days, then perhaps it is going to require of us more than we've ever given. Perhaps a different kind of breaking and willingness is required to unlock the *empathy, compassion, and intercession needed* to bring these fields to harvest. Perhaps when we allow that to happen, we will see the church weeping the tears that will water this harvest to fruit.

There is so much unrest on the planet, and sometimes the church doesn't always respond with the grace and presence needed. I spoke of these things at our 2016 Hillsong Conference in a message carefully titled "Latter Day Tears." I shared with a degree of measure because the subject is not small. In essence, I was challenging the diverse breadth of the gathered church to face the fact that these are not days for being *absent from the scene*. A secular (and oftentimes dismissive) world doesn't always welcome the presence of believers, but when did that ever stop God's Spirit working in the lives of people? Whether the devil likes it or not, the church is on the landscape and she's not going away. We inhabit a world of rising tensions—a world full of fear, a world easily stirred toward intolerance and hatred, a world of increasing xenophobia, a world where racism (of all kinds) sits not far beneath the surface in many nations—so the question I present is: What would God have us do? React, run, hide, judge . . . or bend low with His Spirit and weep for those who are suffering?

I know I have alluded to this already, and in the next chapter I will touch on prayer again, but for the sake of a world drowning in despair, we need to stir empathy. All empathy asks is that we lean in and identify with the difficulty or suffering of another. Empathy is a choice. Christians can turn their backs, switch channels on the television if the issues become too confronting, or as in the Good Samaritan story of old, cross to the other side of the street . . . *or* they can allow the Spirit of God to lead them. When we choose to not quench the Spirit within, and when we allow empathy to lead us, "compassion" will enter the frame. And when compassion enters the frame, the miraculous has a shot, because our hearts are compelled to a deeper response. All I'm suggesting is a heightened willingness to allow the Spirit to prompt and lead. The progression is simple: *eyes wide open, empathy, compassion, intercession (alongside the Spirit), which then unlocks the miraculous!*

A natural field needs both early and latter rain to bring it to maturity—and in the same way the spiritual harvest fields of this world need the early and latter rain to bring them to maturity. I don't know everything, but I do know that the Bible speaks of the *early church and a latter-day church*, and it says that the glory of the latter will exceed the glory of the former. I do know that generations have gone before us, and their tears have softened the ground and paved a way. I do know that first-century Christians gave all for the testimony, and I do know that as I lingered in worship before stepping onto the platform to share these thoughts for the first time, I felt God whisper, *"Bobbie, my ancients gave all . . . they carried their crosses . . . they were crucified in their thousands . . . the earth absorbed their blood, sweat, and tears."* So the question presents: *What shall we be and who shall we be in this generation?* As the generation rising to her stature alongside the Holy Spirit, what will our lives represent? We gather to stadiums and arenas to worship, hold conferences, and encourage one another in faith—our ancient brothers and sisters were gathered to arenas and were fed to wild beasts. Our freedom came with great cost; it is for this freedom that Christ has saved us, and it is for the freedom of others that we must rise also. Allow the integrity of His Spirit to lead you, because someone needs to weep with those who are weeping.

When Hillsong UNITED recorded the *Of Dirt and Grace* album in Israel, the humanitarian organization World Vision took them to the Syria/Lebanon border. They had the honor and heartbreak of experiencing one of the many refugee camps. They tell of entering a tent and listening to a man relate his flight from Syria. He shared how he had lost family along the way, that his brother was dying of treatable diabetes simply because they had no access to medicine. Reduced to silence and with humility of heart, our guys quietly asked, "Forgive us, but in all truthfulness, how do you cope? How do you honestly cope?" With a child in his lap, the man looked up from where he was sitting on the ground and said, "You see that field over there...the desolate field at the end of the camp? *We go there and weep.*"

Friend, the Lord knows you inside out. He knows the thoughts and plans He has toward you and the measure entrusted to make them reality. He knows what disturbs and impassions you and what you are capable of. He is trustworthy to develop every aspect of your life and every inch of your journey according to His will. He also knows how to include you in these fields that are calling your name and which are in desperate need of intervention. Therefore, be attentive.

The road forward weaves itself through all manner of terrain. At times what that road presents is deeply personal. You may feel alone with only the lamp of His Word to guide you. At times the path presents enemies and giants that need to be defeated and chained. At times the way onward will feel carefree and wonderful. Allow me to remind you that this God-centered life is a great life—there is more sunshine and blessing than storm cloud and challenge, but something that is common to all of us is that *wherever these paths wind . . . we find humanity.*

We need to be fully awake. This precious world does not need a church asleep at the wheel, sounding like she is awake but with rhetoric that is dangerous instead of life-giving. She needs a church who is alive, vibrant, relevant, and standing tall along-side society . . . a church with her hand to the plow, her eyes on the ripening field, and an ear attentive to His direction.

NINE

STAY WITHIN THE WONDER AND MYSTERY

(Deep Calls to Deep)

Deep calls to deep at the roar of your waterfalls" (Ps. 42:7 ESV).

Our planning meetings are always fun. We press in around a big boardroom table with another layer of bodies often perched on side cabinets and chairs, affectionately appropriated from anyone foolish enough to leave their desk unattended. Never in the history of our church have we ever had enough office space or quiet corners for the myriad of meetings that take place within our slightly crazed world. This meeting was for Colour. We were possibly six months out from opening night and curtain call, but nevertheless we had to begin early because our ministry is so expansive that it's like orchestrating a landing pattern of planes at London's Heathrow. As my team mingled, joked, and shuffled endless papers, Cassandra entered. As always, what entered the room with Mrs. Langton was a burst of sunshine and positive vibe. The girl has a remarkable capacity. Not only is she my little third heaven comrade in all things creative and prophetic, she also has a remarkable capacity to organize, with relative ease (smile), a creative global community who measure in the thousands.

As we sat down, Cass hardly gave me time to open in prayer and begin the meeting. Our theme for that year was "Be Found in the Mystery." Wide-eyed and expectant, she launched the question, "So, Pastor Bobbie, what does that mean to you... what does 'be found in the mystery' mean to you?" The entire table went silent as if ready to witness a response more profound than Spurgeon, Wesley, Lewis, or Augustine. Hilarious. I'm the girl who was too shy to attend Bible college because the thought of sharing a five-minute chapel message terrified me. I remember pausing. When I'm thinking creatively I always look up and to the right, which is encouraging because apparently that is the creative sphere of your brain (needless to say, I seldom look left because I'm completely pathetic with numbers). As the team waited, I replied slowly and hesitantly, "Well, to me personally, I think the mystery of God is the beauty of the gospel." The silence around the table was not disapproval but rather a palpable sense of release. Demystifying the simple and beautiful gospel was definitely more doable than trying to creatively unravel the mysteries of eternity on a shoestring budget.

Therefore, if my journey could again teach you anything (of all the profound things that could be said on this subject), allow me simply to remind you:

SOME THINGS NEVER GROW OLD

Some things never grow old, friend, because they are, in fact, part of *an eternal mystery that never fades, ages, or diminishes in wonder.* If we are to successfully stay the path, we need these eternal treasures to be vital and growing within our experience. In Colossians, Paul writes of the supremacy of the Son and encapsulates the mystery that has both haunted and held mankind in pursuit of what is deeper and more. It says:

We look at this Son and *see the God* who cannot be seen. We look at this Son and see God's original purpose in everything created. For everything, absolutely everything, above and below, visible and invisible, rank after rank after rank of angels—everything got started in him and finds its purpose in him. He was there before any of it came into existence and holds it all together right up to this moment. And when it comes to the church, he organizes and holds it together, like a head does a body. He was supreme in the beginning and—leading the resurrection parade—he is supreme in the end. From beginning to end he's there, towering far above everything, everyone. So spacious is he, so roomy, that everything of God finds its proper place in him without crowding. Not only that, but all the *broken and dislocated pieces of the universe*—people and things, animals and atoms—get properly fixed and fit together in vibrant harmonies, all because of his death, his blood that poured down from the cross.

You yourselves are a case study of what he does. At one time you all had your backs turned to God, thinking

rebellious thoughts of him, giving him trouble every
chance you got. But now, by giving himself completely at
the cross, actually dying for you, Christ brought you over
to God's side and put your lives together, whole and holy in
his presence. You *don't walk away from a gift like that*! You
stay grounded and steady in that bond of trust, constantly
tuned in to the Message, careful not to be distracted or
diverted. There is no other Message—just this one. Every
creature under heaven gets this same Message. I, Paul, am
a messenger of this Message." (Colossians 1:15–23 MSG;
emphasis mine)

The beauty of the gospel is that the Father chose not to abandon us.

The beauty of the gospel is that the Father, Son, and Holy
Spirit could not bear the thought of us never returning home to
experience all they have prepared.

The beauty of the gospel is that all the broken and dislocated
pieces of our lives can be fixed, because Jesus gave himself completely at the cross.

The magnitude of this redemptive plan is both profound and
humbling to me, and as I shared with the girls (at the conference
we were planning), no one in their right mind walks away from
a gift such as this. I want to encourage you not to allow anything
to dull your senses or passion for what is vital in life. Therefore,
always remember:

Worship never grows old. Worship would have to be the greatest mystery within the mystery of God. In the book of Revelation, chapter 19, John fell at the feet of the angel who had caused

him to see and experience the culmination of time and the literal marriage supper of the Lamb, where every man, woman, and child who has ever responded to the invitation will be welcomed to the table. Scripture says that John fell to worship the one showing him these wonders, but the angel prevented him, saying that he also was a messenger in the same way we are. He said—worship God!

Worship is the personal domain and territory of your heart. It is not a twenty- or thirty-minute set of songs at the front end of a church service—it is the unseen yet felt realm that connects you to the realm of the King of heaven. I cannot judge the depth or sincerity of your worship, in the same way that you cannot judge mine—it issues from a place of surrender, love, and adoration. Be encouraged that the kind of worship that will never grow old or wearisome is worship that *peels back the layers* within your soul, within the atmosphere that surrounds you, and within that holy place where only God Himself dwells. It is worship that breaks down the hard shell that often envelops the human heart. It changes the atmosphere within our homes and churches, and it affects the prevailing spiritual atmosphere over cities, neighborhoods, and nations. And it's worship that gives us entry into the very presence of God Himself.

Psalm 91 calls it a "secret place"—not in the sense that it is hidden or difficult to find, but secret as in a place worthy of being sought and found. A place where you can lean, take refuge, and listen for what is not of this earthly realm. Many years ago, I had a (measured) vision of the throne room. I didn't see the glory or the legions of angels or elders who cry "Holy, holy!" It was more about standing on the perimeters of the room. As I stood, tentatively peeking in and hesitant to enter, I felt the

Holy Spirit draw near. It was as though He was standing on the edges with me. He gently whispered, "You know you can go in, Bobbie…You can go in, sit at His feet, climb on His lap if you want…He will tell you all you need to know." I will never forget that moment. I've shared it often, and will continue to do so if it helps someone understand the tender embrace and invitation of the Father. Worship is our learned art of tapping into the intimacy of His presence.

Genesis 28 records a pivotal encounter in the timeline of mankind. Sojourning Jacob is earthside and in a wilderness setting. He falls asleep and dreams a dream, but what he experiences is more than a mere dream. The account is the first mention in Scripture of the House of God, and the beginning of a greater revelation that God is closer than we know. In his dream, Jacob sees a ladder or staircase rising into the heavens, with the angels of God ascending and descending. In itself, that bears witness of the activity of angels in the realm that surrounds us. God Himself is standing at the top and declares, *"Behold, I am with you."* He also speaks promises to Jacob of his future. Jacob then awakens and declares to himself that God was present all the time, even though his natural eyes could not see. Verses 16 and 17 say:

> And Jacob awoke from his sleep and he said, "Surely the Lord is in this place and I did not know it." He was afraid and said, "How to be feared *and* reverenced is this place! This is none other than the house of God, and this is the gateway to heaven!" (AMPC)

Friend, true worship never gets old, because it taps into a knowing that our magnificent God is closer than we know—"as near as the tongue in your mouth, as close as the heart in your chest" (Rom. 10:8 MSG). I challenge you to stir up a hunger within to know Him more deeply and intimately, to seek and find a God whose wonder is without measure and whose love can never be extinguished. Cultivate your own heart of worship and follow in the steps of the psalmist who said, "Deep calls to deep in the roar of your waterfalls" (Ps. 42:7 NIV). Stir the deep well of salvation within you—allow it to connect with the deep places in God that then attract those thirsting for truth. I am of the belief that in these coming days, people will draw near, and without words being spoken they will sense His presence upon you because you have been with Jesus.

Worship will never grow old to the one whose eyes are set on pilgrimage and whose heart is homesick for the courts of their God (see Ps. 84). It's the language of heaven, and nothing separates us from entering into the praise party and anthem of worship happening even now as you read these words.

Knowing you are called never grows old. Why? Because (again) it is the beckoning of heaven and the beckoning of the fields that I have already written of. Knowing that you are the royal son or daughter of the living God, called for greatness and commission, is something that acts as a holy magnet. It will keep you steadfast upon the path, because there is no way you would ever forfeit such an honor as being called.

Knowing you are royal changes everything. *Behavior changes.* The way you treat people, and the way you allow people to treat you, changes immensely when you know you are of royal descent. The temptation to hurl abuse or the odd fry pan across the room changes when you realize that such behavior is unbe-coming. *Authority changes.* Knowing that the royal blood of Christ is surging through the veins of your spirit-man puts you on a differ-ent playing field when it comes to taking authority over the chal-lenges of life. Born-again status allows you to confidently remind the enemy of whose kingdom you represent. Being *comfortable enough to ask changes* when you know whose child you are. You realize that you are not petitioning a mean God but rather your heavenly Father, who in all truthfulness has already given you the sun, moon, and stars. And being *comfortable in the face of adversity* always changes when you know your royal heritage cannot be sto-len from you. No adversity this side of eternity, no battle won or seemingly lost, has any bearing on what is eternal. Good people in history lost their head, suffered persecution, and died in faith (hav-ing not yet received their promise), and yet we know from Scrip-ture that their final outcome this side of eternity had no bearing on the unshakable kingdom and crown that awaited them.

Christ in us, the hope of glory, is not a pretty or poetic sen-tence in the Bible. It is powerful and compelling truth. I encour-age you to establish these convictions within your own soul, because they will travel you well. Many are called, few are cho-sen. Choose to be chosen, believe that you are the right man or woman in the right place at the right time, and choose to make your life an offering to your King—the reward will always out-weigh the sacrifice (see Col. 1:27 and Matt. 22:14).

The village in need of rescue never grows old. Paul in Colos-sians 2:2 (MSG) continues teaching us of the mystery: "I want you woven into a tapestry of love, in touch with everything there is to know of God."

If we are going to be a people truly in touch with everything there is to know of God, then we have to know His heart toward the lost. I've camped in these thoughts throughout this book, but nevertheless, gorgeous friend, they never get old! There is a famous African proverb, you probably know it well: "*It takes a village to raise a child.*" Well, in my mind, it also takes a village to rescue a village. Earth being the village in need of rescue, and the church being the village with a message of salvation. Earth being a village in crisis—magnificently wonderful on so many levels, yet full of division and trouble on so many other levels.

I shared these thoughts with the girls at my 2016 conference, because there is a world on our watch that desperately needs a message of hope. The desire of God is blessing for all. Never allow complacency to creep into our blessed and "made whole" lives. The promise of blessing for those who follow Him is biblical—"blessed," "fortunate," "happy," and "enviable" are adjectives in Scripture that constantly describe a blessed life. Don't allow misguided critics (or wounded Christians with a chip on their shoulder) to tell you otherwise, implying there is something inherently wrong with the favor that comes with serving God. The reality of poverty in this world does not make the reality of blessing wrong—it only becomes wrong when we as believers lose sight of our responsibility toward the impoverished and suffering in this world. As Brian constantly reminds our church, we are blessed to be a blessing.

Jesus came to reinstate the world to how it should be, so if my journey could add perspective, let's rejoice that we are part of a gospel that is insanely intentional. Let's live *intentional in our desire* to be a tangible blessing to the world around us, and let's rejoice that we are part of a rising church with vision, mission, and growing insight on how to be and bring change. Our work in the field is certainly not yet complete, but let's rejoice to be part of a community with answers in their stride and hand. And ultimately, let's rejoice in a God who is well able to make inroads into people's lives. He did so in my life and yours, so He can certainly do it for others.

Do you have someone in your world desperate for answers? Let's believe that in the days ahead we will witness uncanny miracles in their life.

The greatest weapon of our warfare never grows old. Prayer! I'm pretty confident that prayer ranks high within the landscape of mysteries. Good old-fashioned prayer remains our greatest weapon of warfare against all that is unjust, unfair, and wrong in this world.

Prayer has never gone out of fashion, and I believe that a *renaissance of prayer* is happening on our watch. People are awakening to the power within their armor and arsenal as believers. Being intimate with God allows a person room to present and petition for their own needs and desires, but a different realm of prayer is emerging—a realm where people are discovering that prayer still avails much! A new generation of prayer warriors (men, women, business people, housewives, students, and young people) are discovering that fervent and heartfelt prayer still wears the spiritual enemy down and tempers the battle. They're discovering as mere mortals that they can connect with forces beyond this world and witness divine intervention. They're awakening to the fact that prayer is miraculous in every sense of the word, and a mystery to be pursued. Within my own life (and that of the Sisterhood movement) we are realizing that the *collective, heartfelt, compassionate, authoritative prayer of an awakened church* is capable of miraculous inroads (see James 5:16).

In Matthew 21:13, Jesus echoes the prophetic words of the Old Testament. In a display of zeal, He enters the temple and declares to a New Testament people that His house will be known as a house of prayer for all people. God's heart is exemplified in the words of Isaiah:

> And as for the outsiders *who now follow me*, working for me, loving my name, and wanting to be my servants— all who keep Sabbath and don't defile it, holding fast to my covenant, I'll bring them to my holy mountain and give them joy in my house of prayer. They'll be welcome to worship the same as the "insiders," to bring burnt offerings and sacrifices to my altar. Oh yes, my *house of worship* will be known as a *house of prayer* for all people. (Isaiah 56:6–7 MSG; emphasis mine)

Consider carefully these verses—outsiders, insiders, a holy mountain where there is no exclusion, and a house of worship that will be known as a house of prayer. These words allow room for everyone. No one is excluded. All are welcome. All are invited.

Friend, we are living in a highways-and-byways era—an era of harvest, where God is prepared to draw home any soul whose heart leans toward him. Jesus tells a haunting parable of the great banquet. The invitation was extended to many, yet many chose their distractions above the kingdom, so the master revealed another layer to the invitation: "And the master said to the servant, 'Go out to the highways and hedges and compel people to come in, that my house may be filled. For I tell you, none of those men who were invited shall taste my banquet'" (Luke 14:23–24 ESV).

Other translations include the words "byways" and "country lanes"—in essence, anywhere where humanity waits in need of good news, help, and invitation. The problem in the parable was not in the invitation. It wasn't as though the master (or God) had no friends—the problem was the sin factor that clouds people's ability to perceive how important the invitation is.

God carries no bias or prejudice. He sees us naked and in need of grace. Ephesians 3 outlines the new covenant of inclusion that Christ wrought for all. Those of faith, no faith, or different faith are capable of being drawn to the truth of who Jesus is, and endless testimony on the earth today bears witness to a God who is drawing sons and daughters home from every corner of this world. Interestingly, the Passion translation notates the word "draw" as being similar to hauling a drowning soul from the ocean. I encourage you, as a true follower of Christ, to carry no bias also. We are all citizens of the earth. Sin is the only thing that divides humanity, and those who are going to walk and stay this path effectively (with the integrity of Christ within their gait) have to look through the divides of culture, religion, preference, or taste, in order to see people as Christ sees them. Everybody is worthy of hearing and responding to the gospel.

Testimony, for example, bears witness that multitudes are turning to Christ across the Arab world, with many saying that Jesus has appeared to them personally, whether that be in the war-torn desolation of their homelands or in cities and townships around the world. That piece of information will either delight the heart or mess with the pious, sanctimonious perception of some who think that to be of Arab descent or different faith is cause for judgment and fear. I am not for one minute suggesting that Jesus is not "the way, the truth, and the life," but the greater issue is acceptance of our fellow man. The truth is that regardless of whether one is born in the Americas, the South Pacific, Asia, Africa, Antarctica, the Middle East, or the vast expanse of greater Europe, the invitation to salvation through Christ belongs to all...and that is how we should view the brotherhood of man.

Jesus didn't for one minute ignore the fact that there was evil or spoiled vines in the batch. Matthew 13 tells another parable of harvest, where the enemy sowed tares. By definition, a tare is "injurious wheat." The servants were distressed and asked the master if they should tear up the harvest. He said no. He was afraid that in destroying the (enemy) tares, harm would come to the precious wheat growing to maturity. He told his workers to let them grow together, and when harvest time came, he would take care of it: "Let both grow together until the harvest, and at harvest time I will tell the reapers, 'Gather the weeds first and bind them in bundles to be burned, but gather the wheat into my barn'" (Matt. 13:30 ESV). That is why the Bible commands us to pray for leaders and governments, so that they will have godly wisdom in leading the world through troublesome times.

Revelation records a new song being sung by every tribe, language, people, and nation, because Jesus' blood paid the ransom for all:

And they sang a new song, saying, "Worthy are you...by your blood you ransomed people for God from every tribe and language and people and nation, and you have made them a kingdom and priests to our God, and they shall reign on the earth." (Revelation 5:9–10 esv)

Allow me to share one example of prayer, rescue, and the embracive nature of God.

Within the #middayBABYmidday prayer initiative—an initiative that simply encourages people to set their alarm to midday as a reminder to pray for others—we focus much attention on the plight of those caught in the madness and horror of war, including of course the current Syrian conflict. As my Colour team and I did all to mobilize thousands of women to prayer in the early half of 2016, I received a message from our lead pastor in Germany. As you would know, the world was awakening afresh to the displacement of millions, with many innocent families and children perishing at sea in their frantic bid for freedom. At the time, Europe's borders were being flooded every day with refugees seeking safety—tens of thousands spewing from their homelands onto the highways and byways of Europe's landmass. As thousands of women were mobilized to prayer in the London conference, and as my own heart awakened that indeed the "spiritual boots were on the ground," my beloved spiritual daughter Joanna sent me a text telling me that her constant midday prayer had been, "God, if there are people on boats, in trouble and sinking…then please get them to shore." She continued, telling me that her husband, Freimut, had been speaking in our Düsseldorf campus. As he chatted afterward in the foyer, someone drew his attention to a young woman they had just met in the foyer also. Jo's text read like this:

Bobbie, she was in her early twenties and in very broken English, she told how she and her family had to leave Syria to flee war . . . Their journey involved a boat trip. It was a big boat, and they were sinking. Water was in the boat and they were in the middle of the ocean. They were sinking . . . and then Jesus appeared. He appeared as the captain and everyone saw Him. Hundreds saw Him. And then the boat was at shore . . . in an instant. Apparently when this young Syrian girl arrived in Germany, she and her family sought a church. They came to our Easter services and all made decisions for Jesus.

I don't know how that story affects you, but I find it remarkable and humbling. Who knows if it was the fervent prayer of our little lead pastor in Germany, or the collective prayer of thousands at midday? All we know is that a miracle saved lives, and Jesus (our captain) was in the midst of the miracle. I pray that your own heart will enlarge to the possibilities of prayer and that together we will find our place in a *miraculous tapestry of intervention* being instigated by the Spirit and fueled by our obedience.

STAY LOYAL TO YOUR OWN HEART AND DISTINCTIVE

I cannot do justice to this book without taking a moment to encourage you that your own heart is critical. Therefore:

Stay pure. Remain fiercely pure and loyal to your own heart. Govern it with integrity and responsibility, and don't ever allow it to lead you astray. The wonder, mystery, and journey is only ever spoiled when we allow our heart to *shift in its loyalty* to either God above or the people we are purposed to do life with. My husband, Brian, is a perfect visionary, leader, and shepherd pastor in this context. If ever there has been one prevailing foundation truth that he relentlessly instills into the fabric of our home, family, team, church, and ministry, then it is the condition of the human heart.

Proverbs 3:4 tells us to guard that heart with all diligence, for out of it spring all the issues and parameters of life. Your heart is your wellspring of life (or death). It has the capacity to be magnificently wonderful or deceitfully evil. I'm sure there is plenty of gray space within those two statements, but when it comes to salvation and all things important, there isn't a lot of gray space. We are either hot or cold in our pursuit of righteousness and service (see Rev. 3:15). So if my journey as a minister, wife, and mother can teach you anything, I would say again and again, stay purehearted within the journey. It's purity of heart that enables you to see God, and nothing gives more stunning expression to this than the 24th Psalm of David:

> The earth is the LORD's and the fullness thereof, the world and those who dwell therein, for he has founded it upon the seas and established it upon the rivers. Who shall ascend the hill of the LORD? And who shall stand in his holy place? He who has clean hands and a pure heart, who does not lift up his soul to what is false and does not swear deceitfully. He will receive blessing from the LORD and righteousness from the God of his salvation. Such is the generation of those who seek him, who seek the face of the God of Jacob. Selah.

Lift up your heads, O gates! And be lifted up, O ancient doors, that the King of glory may come in. Who is this King of glory? The LORD, strong and mighty, the LORD, mighty in battle! Lift up your heads, O gates! And lift them up, O ancient doors, that the King of glory may come in. Who is this King of glory? The LORD of hosts, he is the King of glory! Selah. (Psalm 24 ESV)

Clean hands and pure heart—the two are inseparable if we are going to live as disciples of the King of glory... *clean hands* before Jesus and clean hands in context of those around us... *pure heart* before our King and purity of soul and agenda toward those around us. The cross bears witness! My son isn't the first in history to see the story within the humble beams that bore the Son of God, but in the *Let Hope Rise* movie, Joel sits on a stool in an empty warehouse and gives expression to how the cross is a picture of what this world needs. The vertical and horizontal beams bore the broken and bleeding body of our Savior as He made the ultimate sacrifice. As our stance continues to be upright and vertical in focus, then our stance horizontally will continue to be (and become) the reach that Christ needs from us. Purity of heart enables you to see God—in essence that is what Psalm 24 says: The pure in heart shall see God, and as you do, His presence will continue to change you from glory to glory (see 2 Cor. 3:18). It is in this ongoing and daily transformation that the miracles happen.

Therefore, keep short accounts with Jesus and let the Word and His Spirit constantly umpire your heart. Don't allow the sun to go down on your anger. The Bible says, "Be angry, but sin not" (Eph. 4:26)—there's a fine line of difference there. Always serve the Lord with gladness, and don't let anyone or anything spoil your joy. Your joy is your well of salvation, deep calling to deep. Remain evenly yoked and of one spirit with the bride or groom of your youth. Stay in step with those you labor with in the field, and allow no little foxes or wedges to spoil the vine and divide what unites. Remember always that it is the spirit (and purity) of unity that attracts the commandment of blessing from the Father. Be generous even as your Father in heaven is generous. Be uncomplicated and low maintenance as a person—be the friend, colleague, or partner who isn't easily offended and who looks at life from higher ground. And above all else, play only ever to an audience of one. Others will always be observing your life, and hopefully they will imitate you as you imitate Christ, but always remember, friend, there is only one true audience, and His name is Jesus. Do that and Abba Father will be pleased. And remember always, the Holy Spirit is constantly alongside with "wind words," strength, and the occasional nudge (or shove) to enable you to stay on track and purehearted to the end.

And if I would say one more thing:

Stay true to your own distinctive. Not only as an individual but also as a church or ministry. We glean from one another, we inspire one another to greatness and often lift the bar to greater possibilities and heights in God, but don't copycat others. Our distinctives in calling are common in one sense—we all want to serve God and make His fame known, but know and walk in your own *grace zone*. There is nothing worse than someone who tries to mimic the ministry of someone else or, more important, the anointing upon another. As a church, we clearly recognize the distinctive that God has entrusted and anointed us in. We steward that anointing carefully, and as we steward it, it has continued to flow. Perhaps I will save these insights for the revised version, *Heaven Is in This House* (one day, someday, right?). Stay within the gold of who you are, not some brass-value imitation. You have something unique to bring to the table, and as I have labored intensely to say . . . you really are a fabulous garden, vineyard, and gift waiting to happen for more people than you can imagine. Why such confidence? Because multitudes are in the valley of decision right now, and Jesus needs every man, woman, and child, present and accountable.

My glorious word count within this book is almost exhausted (How is that possible? she asks with wide-eyed wonder and a smile!). Turn the page and allow me to close this part of the journey with something that will hopefully infuse your steps on this pathway that we must stay loyal and fierce upon.

TEN

STAY THE PATH

(The Epilogue—Chasing Daylight)

As I begin this chapter, I've been awake since before dawn, mindful of what words to leave you with and mindful of my creative colleagues on the other side of the world, chasing all sorts of wonder for what lies ahead in our calendar.

If you recall, I began this book with blank page, full heart, and the hope that my journey could add to yours. I sincerely hope that these words have done that in some way or another. As a writer, I find introductions and epilogues interesting. In many ways, an "introduction" is a combination of greeting and conversation. With those who know your voice and can picture the reality of your life, it's relatively comfortable, and hopefully everything you share resonates with the person they know you to be. However, with those who are new to your voice or experience, the process is a little different. Connection hinges on a number of dynamics, but for the most part any new relationship takes time to develop into what will be a meaningful friendship. I hope our introduction and conversation within these pages has gone the distance and produced a sense of friendship—I've certainly fallen for you as I've been writing.

On the other hand, I find "epilogues" equally intriguing to write. There's a little sadness attached because it feels like a farewell, and there is an underlying tension to bring the matter to a worthy conclusion. I've only written a few in my lifetime, but I choose to think of them like a comma in a good sentence or that moment in conversation where you say, "Hey, friend, it's been awesome, but I have to go... I'll see you again soon, though."

CHASING DAYLIGHT

The colleagues I just mentioned are in China, filming and taking photos for my upcoming women's conference. I'm not quite sure how they managed to fit China into their somewhat minimal creative budget, but being the innovative team they are, they did—and I'm certainly not going to quench their faith and deep desire to serve the dream when it comes to the daughters of sweet planet Earth.

As I sit here at my desk, text messages (from them) are popping up on my screen, creating no end of endearing distraction. They're weary because (to my shock and concern) they found themselves in a rural hospital the night before, with strange eye infections and mild electrocution (another story for another time), but had still gotten up at four a.m. to scale a certain range of mountains. The theme they're laboring to capture is that of *being found in the field*. The mandate of Colour is to place value upon womanhood, in order that women can rise

up in their various fields of life and calling and place value upon
humanity. Not a small vision (smile), but nevertheless it has
become a movement of world changers over the past twenty
years.

I'm telling you all this because as I sit here (in California) trying to give expression to a picture of eternity in my spirit, they're
on a mountaintop in Guangxi Province trying to capture the
same desire on film. They're giving all to find the dawn light and
chase haunting sunsets because they know their little senior pastor has a fascination with the romance of a King who will one
day return. Friend, one day this world as we know it will end.
One day the Father will motion toward His only begotten and
beloved Son and say, "Today, son . . . today." One day the heavens will peel back and the testimony they have borne for several
millennia will be over. One day our Bridegroom and champion,
Jesus Christ, will appear and the glorious day spoken of and
yearned for by millions will be upon us. I don't want to frighten
anyone (perish that thought!) but that day will come, whether
in our lifetime or not and regardless of readiness. One day the
sun will set and a new day will dawn . . . the day of His coming.
And the challenge is to be ready.

Psalm 19 tells how the heavens speak of God's glory and presence and how the natural sun can be likened to the Son of God
who will one day emerge and appear to all. I guess my little team
and I are simply trying to capture these truths for those whose
eyes have yet to fully comprehend what surrounds them.

The heavens declare the glory of God; the skies proclaim
the work of his hands. Day after day they pour forth
speech; night after night they reveal knowledge. They

have no speech, they use no words; no sound is heard from them. Yet their voice goes out into all the earth, their words to the ends of the world. In the heavens God has pitched a tent for the sun. It is like a bridegroom coming out of his chamber, like a champion rejoicing to run his course. It rises at one end of the heavens and makes its circuit to the other; nothing is deprived of its warmth. (Psalm 19:1–6 NIV)

THE ROMANCE AND CHALLENGE

The *endless romance* that I am constantly seeking to give expression to is of a coming King whose love and warmth are for all humankind. And the *endless challenge* that consumes my heart is that people will "stay the path" and experience, at all cost, what He has secured for them, that they'll awaken to a glorious calling that allows them to confidently occupy the landscape surrounding their everyday life, with a willingness to help others prepare for the day when they also will enter eternity. Psalm 84 promises blessing to those who understand this, and it speaks of a pilgrimage that will one day culminate with God (in all His fullness) coming into full view. It speaks of a people triumphant to the end.

And how blessed all those in whom you live, whose lives become roads you travel; They wind through lonesome valleys, come upon brooks, discover cool springs and pools brimming with rain! God-traveled, these roads curve up the mountain, and at the last turn—Zion! God in full view! God of the Angel Armies, listen: O God of Jacob, open your ears—I'm praying! Look at our shields, glistening in the sun, our faces, shining with your gracious anointing. One day spent in your house, this beautiful place of worship, beats thousands spent on Greek island beaches. I'd rather scrub floors in the house of my God than be honored as a guest in the palace of sin. All sunshine and sovereign is GOD, generous in gifts and glory. He doesn't scrimp with his traveling companions. It's smooth sailing all the way with GOD of the Angel Armies. (Psalm 84:5–12 MSG)

The image of Zion—a glorious city of wonder that will light up the sky for all to see—is an irresistible thought. I love that there is a holy mountain that welcomes all, and that our God is indeed God of the Angel Armies! I love that He watches over His traveling companions, and that this journey through life can be smooth sailing, not because ocean waters are always calm, but because there is a faithful captain of our souls. And I love the thought of shields glistening in the sun!

Friend, when you settle within yourself that you are *called, anointed, and armed* for this journey through life—whether in the realm of life, love, or leadership—nothing has the capacity to knock you off the path or steal what is yours in Christ. You will arrive safely, with those gathered and intended to travel with you...and your shield of calling (and warfare) will glisten in the light of His glory. I am perhaps waxing poetic, but I have a vision that haunts me in a beautiful way: I see the church of our Lord Jesus Christ, advancing throughout the earth with the sunlight of His presence reflecting off our lives and acting as a beacon of light to those in darkness. There are multitudes in the (darkened) valleys of decision in need of someone to guide them to freedom. Don't underestimate who you are, or the power of God's goodness within you. Your witness of faith can become a shield of hope and protection for others. What God has invested within you is critical to the path we are all on, because we're in this together. The church will only mature into the glorious lighthouse she is created to be because of the unified strength of those who carry His Name!

A MOUNTAIN SONG

My inherent desire with this book is simply to encourage you along your pathway and journey. Keep your boots in the soil of the fields you are called to, keep your eyes on the dawn light of that approaching day, and keep the flame of His love burning bright within. Don't let anything disqualify you or trick you into being unprepared when the Bridegroom comes. The ancient psalmist wrote, "Your statutes have been my songs in the house of my pilgrimage" (Ps. 119:54 NKJV). Allow His statutes to become the defining song and testimony of your life. My own sons are not ancient psalmists, but Joel and Matt Crocker wrote a song a few years ago called "Mountain." I could have chosen any song to close with, but allow me to put a "comma" on this book with these beautiful lyrics, and then share a little story that I believe the Spirit of God would have me share.

> *See a light in the darkness*
> *A city shining without a veil*
> *This hill becoming a mountain*
> *A solid rock that will never fail*

Your Name
My hope
Fortress in the raging storm
My heart
Is Your home
Jesus let Your love take hold

The Stone the builders rejected
Laid to ransom a fractured bride
Our crushing weight on Your shoulders
You stand forever with arms stretched wide

For Your Name, heart and soul
My life is Yours a living stone
For Your glory, heart and soul
Surrendered all to build a home

Your Name, my sure foundation
The Hope of glory for one and all
Your love endures forever
A holy mountain that will not fall

All the earth welcome home
In every heart Your will be done
All creation welcome home
This hope is ours, Your kingdom come

We cry holy, holy, holy
We cry holy is Your Name

For Your name, heart and soul
My life is Yours a living stone
For Your glory, heart and soul
Surrendered all to build a home
—"MOUNTAIN," WORDS
AND MUSIC BY MATT
CROCKER AND JOEL
HOUSTON, 2012

BRANDON'S STORY

My friend was only thirty-two when tragedy struck. At the time, she and her husband had three young sons within their loving household and were pastoring in a part of the United States where temperatures soar and cacti dominate the desert landscape. I didn't know her personally when the accident happened, but Brian and I had heard of this stoic couple, grieving the loss of their young son Brandon. He was nine years old. In the path of grief was an older brother, Austin, and Brandon's twin brother, Bryant.

I asked permission to share M'lisa and Kevin's story, because it's deeply personal. They told me that they had been trying to write of it themselves for many years, and that my unexpected request had served as a prompt to push through and finish doing so. Nevertheless, they gave me permission.

M'lisa not only suffered the loss of her son in the accident, she was also severely injured herself. She had broken five vertebrae in her back and neck. Her face was crushed to the extent that surgeons had to harvest bone from her skull to rebuild it. She told me that the doctors cut her from ear to ear twice within the following eighteen months, in an effort to reconstruct her broken facial structure. Because of her extensive injuries, including those to her spine, she was unable to be with the family as they gathered in the hospital to say good-bye to her little boy. For the funeral, she was given a two-hour pass and attended in an ambulance and body cast. She was unable to go to the graveside.

One night several months later, she said, the pain in her heart was unbearable. I don't know if you have suffered grief of any kind, but the pain can be excruciating. It can consume a person's entire being—body, soul, spirit, emotions, everything—and little outside of time and God's grace can heal it. I know because I lost my precious father when I was young, and the only relief I found was when the Holy Spirit came alongside me as a three-week-old new Christian. He told me that the Savior I had just encountered bore not only my sins upon the cross but also my grief and sorrow. As I lay sobbing on my bedroom floor, He gently whispered, "Now let Him lift the pain."

M'lisa told me that her pain was unspeakable. She said that in some ways her inconsolable grief was that she had not had a chance to hold her son and say good-bye. She knew he was in a better place and that he was safe, yet her mother heart felt torn by the separation. All she wanted was closure—a moment to kiss him good-bye and run her hands through his soft curls one more time. As she cried herself to sleep one night, she tells how Father God gave her a miraculous and supernatural gift. In her words:

"I was awakened by a knock at the back door of our home. As I opened the door, it felt as though my heart stopped. I was looking into the beautiful blue eyes of my precious boy Brandon, standing arms outstretched to embrace and love on his heartbroken mommy. I grabbed him and carried him over to the couch. I looked at him with tears and said, 'I've missed you so much…I just want to be with you.' He said, 'I know, Mommy, but it will just be a lil' while and we will be together forever!' I said, 'I know, I just miss you now!'

"I looked intensely into his eyes and asked, 'How are you?' I have been raised in church my entire life and I've heard all the stories of how great heaven is…how the streets are of gold and gates are made of pearls. I knew Brandon was in the presence of Jesus, but he still needed his mommy! All I could see was my little boy walking on those streets of gold alone, wandering and wondering where his mommy was! As I looked at Brandon's face, there was a bright glow about him. As he answered me, his face lit up and he beamed, 'Oh, Mommy, it is sooooo wonderful! I can't even tell you how amazing and wonderful it is!'

"I had *never* seen my baby's smile that big (and he had a smile that lit up a room). This was different. He radiated a light…a *joy* so tangible that I have never experienced anything like it before or since! It was in that very moment that my heart was overwhelmed with the peace of God that assured me my baby was okay! Nothing on this earth could ever give him what he was experiencing in this glorious place…he was now truly home!

"In one moment, God had given me the closure I had been yearning and praying for. I swept him up in my arms and kissed his little face…sang to him…and ran my fingers through his soft blond curls. After some time, the sun started to rise, and he said, 'Mommy, I have to go…' He said when the sun came up, he had to go back. So I walked him to the back door and kissed him good-bye, and as soon as I shut the door, I awoke! At first, I lay in bed in disbelief that it had only been a dream, but it truly felt like I had been in the presence of my son! I had felt his face and soft curls and smelled his sweet fragrance. I know I had been given the gift of holding my son again. I will forever be grateful for God's unwavering love toward me, and His heart to heal every broken place in our lives."

M'lisa and Kevin's family has grown, and I see them now with a growing handful of grandbabies in their lives. M'lisa is the sweetest person and as pretty as a picture. You would never be aware of her injuries without someone telling you. I don't know why I returned to this story, but I'm sure the Holy Spirit brought it back into view for a reason. Perhaps you've lost a child or loved one and the pain still consumes you. Take courage from this story and that of King David (the ancient psalmist I keep quoting). He lost a child also, and then one day his grief lifted and he declared that while the child could not return to him, he could and would go to the child. David penned revelation of a world in heaven that awaits us all if we have a heart to believe.

The world is full of stories of divine intervention and visitation like the one I just shared. Who are we to judge another's experience or dream, because the Bible is full of those who encountered truth within the *dreamscape* of their life? I've shared a few within these pages. I have no difficulty leaning into Brandon's story, because it totally sounds like the Father I know and love. Just like Jesus to do something like that. He's closer than we all know, and only a thin veil separates us—He hears our heartache and prayers, and His love is a never-ending world of surprises.

As I bring these pages to a close, I exhort you to stay the path at all cost. A glorious homecoming awaits you, and it's worth every step. My Jesus is with you. Trust in His goodness because He is the one true Shepherd who will never fail or forsake you. And while daylight remains, let's remember our work in the field is not done.

Jeremiah of old said, "Thus says the LORD: 'Stand by the roads, and look, and ask for the ancient paths, where the good way is; and walk in it, and find rest for your souls'" (Jer. 6:16 ESV).

Be safe and be strong. May your steps lead you perfectly and may the kiss of heaven be upon all that your hand finds to do.

Always and forever,
Bobbie

THE COLOUR CONFERENCE

The 'Colour Your World Women's Conference' started in 1997 and is hosted by Bobbie Houston and the global Hillsong Church team. It flows from the heart of Hillsong's local Sisterhood ministry where women from every age and walk of life gather. At its core, the conference exists to place value upon womanhood and champion the potential within women everywhere. Bobbie and the Hillsong team currently host this conference in Sydney, London, Kiev, Cape Town, and in multiple cities across the USA.

The COLOUR Conference is much more than an annual event that gathers thousands of women; it is an ever-growing global movement of everyday women seeking to create a stance for justice, change and influence. Our team labour to create an atmosphere that will refresh heart and soul and inspire transformation. Our desire is that worship, creativity and the presentation of God's Word (the Bible) will honour the King of heaven and cause faith to rise, enabling the enormous potential within to become reality. The conference is continually creating pathways for women to raise awareness and mobilize response.

The Colour story is one of "divine grace" and it's ability to find its way into the human heart and weave the story of God's great love into the lives of those seeking a better world.

"For God SO LOVED the world that He gave His one and only Son – that whoever believes in him shall not perish, but have eternal life" (John 3:16)

FOR MORE INFORMATION VISIT COLOURCONFERENCE.COM

THE SISTERHOOD

'Sisterhood' is a term that reflects the heart and spirit of a rising generation of women around the world. Age, background and culture are proving no barrier to this emerging and beautiful movement. Everyday women from every corner of the earth are leaning into the revelation that they are indeed daughters of a living and loving God, and that as His daughters, they carry a capacity and authority to bring change in an ever-challenging and needful world.

Defined by genuine empathy, the influence of this host of world-changers is being felt in local and global contexts - from endeavours that bring care to the fragile in local communities, through to the global issues of human trafficking and poverty.

At the core of Sisterhood is a message of value, and a genuine desire to 'unite in friendship and cause', in order to bring hope where hope has been lost. The spirit of sisterhood is seen and felt in the fervent prayer of thousands of women who faithfully uphold nations where injustice and darkness rage out of control. It is seen and felt in young women being inspired by the wisdom and grace of their mothers and the women ahead of them in this journey of life. It is seen and felt in the relentless networking of everyday girls in their local neighbourhoods and in places of influence, as they raise awareness and find solutions for the suffering, forgotten and abused of this world.

There are many pages and chapters within the story of God's daughters on the earth, and as the 'I AM SISTERHOOD' declaration states, we find ourselves in our own 'here and now' with more pages yet to be written and experienced. For insight into the breadth of the Colour Sisterhood, go online and peruse through the various humanitarian initiatives and 500 PROJECT responses. Together we can make a difference.

COLOURSISTERHOOD.COM

THE SISTERHOOD BOOK
AVAILABLE AT BOBBIEHOUSTON.COM

INVEST IN YOURSELF, FAMILY AND FRIENDS
The Sisterhood is a memoir and leadership book capturing the spirit of a global sisterhood.

For more information, resource and to stay up to date with Bobbie Houston,
Hillsong Church and The Colour Sisterhood visit **bobbiehouston.com** or connect
through social media below.

Follow Bobbie on Twitter: **@bobbiehouston** / **@coloursistahood**
Follow Bobbie on Instagram: **@bobbiehouston** / **@coloursisterhood**
Like Brian and Bobbie on Facebook: **fb.com/brianandbobbie** / **fb.com/coloursisterhood**

PODCASTS

Each and everyday, people are accessing free audio podcasts from Bobbie Houston. These
messages are created to bring hope and encouragement to women young and old with practical
and biblical teaching. Your work life, home life and relationships matter to God – and they
matter to us. Join in with others from around the world to receive free teaching that will unlock
and unleash you to your greatest potential.

To access and subscribe to these life-giving messages, search for "Bobbie Houston" in the
iTunes Store or Podcast App.